Speaking Thai

Sunthorn Kohtbantau

ASIA BOOKS

Published and Distributed by
Asia Books Co. Ltd.,
5 Sukhumvit Road Soi 61,
PO Box 40,
Bangkok 10110,
Thailand.
Tel: (66) 0-2715-9000 ext. 3202–4
Fax: (66) 0-2714-2799
E-mail: information@asiabooks.com
Web site: asiabooks.com

Typeset by COMSET Limited Partnership

Printed in Thailand by Darnsutha Press Co., Ltd.

ISBN 974-8303-24-1

สารบาญ　　　Sǎ-râ-b<u>a</u>n　　　Contents

v

Preface

This *Speaking Thai* book is written for foreigners who speak languages other than Thai, and wish to learn how to speak Thai. It is especially for tourists who plan to spend some time in the Kingdom of Thailand. However, those foreigners who have just come and have already begun working in Thailand, and wish to learn to speak Thai, are not left out in the design of each lesson.

Accordingly, the book has 10 lessons, and each lesson has four main parts: Conversation, Vocabulary, Grammar Points, and Exercises. The Conversation part is a dialogue between two persons, A and B, during various activities that tourists and foreigners are expected to do while in Thailand. The Vocabulary part builds up vocabulary with correct tones and exact pronunciation. Some words are repeated in many lessons, indicating their frequency of usage in speaking.

The Grammar Points part is for those who wish to study in detail some basic principles of the language. Each lesson includes a few grammar points on words and expressions. Finally, the Exercises part is for those who wish to build up words, phrases and sentences for improving their speaking. The exercises are drawn from the preceding three parts so that words, phrases, sentences, and other grammar points can be repeated, practiced and brought into use with ease.

It is recommended that the Vocabulary part be covered before going back to the Conversation part, followed by the Grammar Points and the Exercises.

For a good command of spoken Thai, the learner should not skip the Exercises. And before going on to other lessons, please spend some time on "Important Features of Thai" on (pages 6-12 of the First Lesson).

This book can be used as a self-study material for adult learners, or with a teacher.

Good luck to everybody!

Dr. Sunthorn Kohtbantau

บทที่ 1	Bòd Tî-nùeng	The First Lesson
ที่ด่านตรวจคน	Tî Dàn Trùad	At Immigration
เข้าเมือง	Kon-Kâo-M<u>uea</u>ng	

1. บทสนทนา / Bòd Sŏn-tâ-n<u>a</u> / Conversation

1) ก: สวัสดีครับ

Sà-wàd-d<u>i</u> Krâb

Hello.

ข: สวัสดีค่ะ

Sà-wàd-d<u>i</u> Kâ

Hello.

2) ก: คุณพูดไทยได้ไหม

Kun P<u>û</u>d Tâi Dâi Măi?

Can you speak Thai?

ข: ค่ะ ดิฉันพูดได้นิดหน่อยค่ะ

Kâ, Dì-chăn Pûd Dâi Nîd-nàwy Kâ

Yes, I can speak a little.

3) ก: ขอต้อนรับสู่ประเทศไทย

Kăw T âwn-râb Sù Prà-têd-tai

Welcome to Thailand.

ข: ขอบคุณมากค่ะ

Kàwb-kun Mâg Kâ

Thank you very much.

4) ก: ขอดูหนังสือเดินทางครับ

Kăw Du Năng-sŭe-doen-tang Krâb

Let me see your passport, please.

ข: นี่ค่ะ

Nî Kâ

Here you are.

5) ก: ขอดูตั๋วเครื่องบินด้วย

Kăw Du T ŭa Krûeang-bin Dûay

May I see the plane ticket as well?

ข: อยู่ที่นี่

Yù Tî-nî

Here it is.

6) ก: คุณอยู่เมืองไทยได้หนึ่งเดือน

Kun Yù Mueang-tai Dâi Nùeng Duean

You can stay one month in Thailand.

ข: ค่ะ ดิฉันจะอยู่กรุงเทพฯ หนึ่งสัปดาห์

Kâ, Dì-chăn Jà Yù Grung-têb Nùeng Sàb-da

Yes, I will stay a week in Bangkok.

7) ก: คุณจะพักที่ไหน

Kun Jà Pâg Tî-nǎi?

Where will you stay?

ข: ที่โรงแรมวายเอ็มซีเอ

Tî Rong-raem Way Em Si E

At YMCA Hotel.

8) ก: โชคดีครับ

Chôk-di Krâb

Good luck, madam.

ข: โชคดีค่ะ

Chôk-di Kâ

Good luck, sir.

2. คำศัพท์ / Kam-sàb / Vocabulary

สวัสดี	Sà-wàd-di	hello, good morning, good afternoon, etc.
ครับ	Krâb	yes, sir or madam; please (used by males)
ค่ะ	Kâ	yes, sir or madam; please (used by females)
พูด	Pûd	speak
ไทย	Tai	Thai
ได้	Dâi	can
ไหม	Mǎi	a question word for yes/no answers
นิดหน่อย	Nîd-nàwy	a little

ขอ...	Kǎw....	let...; may I....?
ต้อนรับ	T âwn-râb	welcome
สู่	Sù	to, towards
ประเทศไทย	Prà-têd-tai	Thailand
ขอบคุณ	Kàwb-kun	thank you
มาก	Mâg	very, much, very much
ดู	Du	see, have a look
หนังสือเดินทาง	Nǎng-sǔe-doen-tang	passport
ตั๋วเครื่องบิน	T ǔa Krûeang-bin	plane ticket
นี่, ที่นี่	Nî, Tî-nî	here
คุณ	Kun	you
อยู่	Yù	stay
เมืองไทย	Mueang-tai	Thailand (spoken word for 'Thailand')
หนึ่ง	Nùeng	one
เดือน	Duean	month
ดิฉัน	Dì-chǎn	I (used by females)
จะ	Jà	will
กรุงเทพฯ	Grung-têb	Bangkok
สัปดาห์	Sàb-da	week
พัก	Pâg	stay
ที่ไหน	Ti-nǎi	where
ที่	Tî	at
โรงแรม	Rong-raem	hotel
วายเอ็มซีเอ	Way Em Si E	YMCA

โชคดี	Chôk-dị	good luck, lucky
บท	Bòd	lesson
ที่หนึ่ง	Tî-nùeng	first
ด่านตรวจคน	Dàn Trùad-kon-	immigration
เข้าเมือง	kâo-mueang	

3. หลักไวยากรณ์ / Lǎg Wai-ya-gawn / Grammar Points

1) สวัสดี Sà-wàd-dị; a greeting word:

   (1) Good morning, good afternoon, good evening, good night, good-bye, so long, etc.

   (2) Hello

สวัสดีครับ	Sà-wàd-di Krâb
สวัสดีค่ะ	Sà-wàd-di Kâ

2) ครับ Krâb:

   (1) Yes, used by males

   (2) Sir, madam, to show politeness

สวัสดีครับ	Sà-wàd-di Krâb
	Hello, sir.
คุณพักที่ไหนครับ	Kun Pâg Tî-nǎi Krâb
	Where do you stay, madam?

3) ค่ะ Kâ:

   (1) Yes, used by females

   (2) Sir, madam, to show politeness

สวัสดีค่ะ	Sà-wàd-di Kâ
	Good morning, sir.
ดิฉันจะพักที่โรงแรม	Dì-chǎn Jà Pâg Tî Rong-raem
	I will stay at a hotel.

4) ดิฉัน Dì-chǎn: I, me, used by females

ดิฉันจะอยู่ที่นี่หนึ่งสัปดาห์

Dì-chăn Jà Yù Tî-ni Nùeng Sàb-da

I will stay here a week.

ดิฉันพูดได้นิดหน่อยค่ะ

Dì-chăn Pûd Dâi Nîd-nàwy kâ

I can speak a little.

5) คุณ Kun: you, used as a polite word to stranger(s), friends, and neighbours, etc.

คุณพูดไทยได้ไหม

Kun Pûd Tai Dâi Măi?

Can you speak Thai?

คุณจะพักที่ไหน

Kun Jà Pâg Tî-năi?

Where will you stay?

6) ขอ... Kăw: Let..., May I...

ขอดูหนังสือเดินทางครับ

Kăw Du Năng-sŭe-doen-tang Krâb

Let me see your passport, please.

ขอดูตั๋วเครื่องบินด้วย

Kăw Du T ŭa Krûeang-bin Dûay?

May I see the plane ticket as well?

4. Important Features of Thai

There are some special features of Thai that readers should know in order to use this book more effectively as follows:

1) **Monosyllabic Language.** Thai is a mono-syllabic language. One-syllable words have meanings. The spellings are simple. If there are some compound words and endings with many letters, they are

combined with other one-syllable words or derived from other languages, especially Pali and Sanskrit languages, through the influence of Buddhism and Hinduism.

2) **Tonal Language.** Thai has fixed tones for all words. No matter whether they are at the beginning or the ending of a sentence, in statements or questions, they still have the same tones.

There are 5 tones in Thai. In this book, the symbols created to represent them are as follows:

<u>Mid Tone</u>	(_)	Mi̱	Pa̱e̱ng	Ra̱-ka̱
<u>Low Tone</u>	(`)	Kà̱w	Nùeng	Hòg
<u>Falling Tone</u>	(^)	Tî-nî̱	Hâ̱	Gâo
<u>High Tone</u>	(´)	Chái	Ní̱	Nán
<u>Rising Tone</u>	(ˆ)	Pŏm	Sǎ̱wng	Sǎ̱m

If mispronounced with exact tones, the meanings are different. Please read the following sentences:

1. Mǎ Má Ma Tî-nî̱.

   The dog (and) the horse come here.

2. Krai Kǎy Kài Gài?

   Who sells hen eggs?

3. Mái Mài Yù̱ Nai Nán Mâi Mǎi?

   Has the new wood in that (place) burnt?

4. Mái Mài Mâi Mâi, Mǎi Mâi.

   The new wood was not burnt, silk burnt.

3) **Consonants.** There are 42 consonants currently used in present-day Thai. Most of them are original consonants, but a few are additional ones added later through the influence of Pali and Sanskrit.

These consonants are classified into 3 groups according to the tones they can produce in words with long vowels and tone marks. The three groups of consonants are as follows:

Group 1: Mid Consonants. There are 7 original consonants and 2 additional consonants. The additional consonants are in brackets.

G<u>aw</u>	ก		G	as in go, get, gone
J<u>aw</u>	จ		J	as in Jack, John, Jane
D<u>aw</u>	ด	(ฎ)	D	as in do, did, done
T<u>aw</u>	ต	(ฏ)	T	as in stand, study, stone
B<u>aw</u>	บ		B	as in book, born, baby
P<u>aw</u>	ป		P	as in Spain, speak, Spanish
A<u>w</u>	อ		O	as in law, daughter, born

Notes: The letter 'T' with a line underneath, T, is ต T <u>aw</u>

The letter 'P' with a line underneath, P, is ป P <u>aw</u>

The letter อ A<u>w</u> is also a semi-vowel.

Group 2: High Consonants. There are 7 original consonants and 3 additional consonants. The additional consonants are in brackets.

Kǎ<u>w</u>	ข		K	as in car, cake, kill
Chǎ<u>w</u>	ฉ		Ch	as in chair, child, chain
Tǎ<u>w</u>	ถ	(ฐ)	T	as in tea, test, tan
Pǎ<u>w</u>	ผ		P	as in pen, pain, pay
Fǎ<u>w</u>	ฝ		F	as in fund, free, coffee
Sǎ<u>w</u>	ส	(ศ,ษ)	S	as in sea, see, seen
Hǎ<u>w</u>	ห		H	as in him, hen, her

Note: The tone of these high consonants is the <u>rising tone</u>, which is the same as the sound of last words in <u>questions</u> expecting yes/no answers. Examples:

(1) Is it your car?

(2) May I have a cup of tea?

(3) Have you seen him?

Group 3: Low Consonants. There are 14 original consonants and 9 additional consonants. The additional consonants are in brackets.

K<u>aw</u>	ค	(ฆ)	K	as in king, kill, keep
Ng<u>aw</u>	ง		NG	as in sing, ring, song
Ch<u>aw</u>	ช	(ฌ)	CH	as in chain, child, chin
S<u>aw</u>	ซ		S	as in see, saw, seen
T<u>aw</u>	ท	(ฑ,ฒ,ธ)	T	as in ten, table, talk
N<u>aw</u>	น	(ณ)	N	as in no, not, nine
P<u>aw</u>	พ	(ภ)	P	as in paper, pay, pen
F<u>aw</u>	ฟ		F	as in food, for, fund
M<u>aw</u>	ม		M	as in man, me, money
Y<u>aw</u>	ย	(ญ)	Y	as in yellow, Yale, yoke
R<u>aw</u>	ร		R	as in raw, red, room
L<u>aw</u>	ล	(ฬ)	L	as in lady, learn, law
W<u>aw</u>	ว		W	as in war, we, win
H<u>aw</u>	ฮ		H	as in hook, hen, hotel

To sum up, the consonants used in this book are as follows:

B	บ		
CH	ฉ		ช (ฌ)
D	ด	(ฎ)	
F	ฝ		ฟ

G	ก			
H	ห		ฮ	
J	จ			
K	ข		ค	(ฆ)
L	ล	(ฬ)		
M	ม			
N	น	(ณ)		
NG	ง			
P	ผ		พ	(ภ)
P̱	ป			
R	ร			
S	ส	(ศ,ษ)	ซ	
T	ถ		ท	(ฑ,ฒ,ธ)
Ṯ	ต	(ฏ)		
W	ว			
Y	ย	(ญ)		

4) **Vowels.** There are 28 vowels currently used in Thai. In this book the symbols and English equivalents are as follows:

a	-ะ	a	as in but, hut, nut
a̱	-า	a	as in bar, car, father
i	̀ -	i	as in bin, win, thin
i̱	́ -	i	as in been, seen, mean
ue	̆ -	-	(No English equivalent, but in German dünn, Münd)
u̱e	̄ -	-	(No English equivalent, but in German Müller, Ubüng)
u	- ̦	u	as in cook, hook, book

10

u	ฺ ู	u	as in food, good, mood
e	เ-ะ	e	as in when, den, then
e	เ-	e	as in well, sell, pain
ae	แ-ะ	a	as in bat, cat, mat
ae	แ-	a	as in bad, mad, sad
o	โ-ะ	o	as in only
o	โ-	o	as in phone, told, sold
aw	เ-าะ	o	as in not, dot, hot
aw	-อ	o	as in law, or, nor
am	-ำ	-	as in umbrella, number
ai	ไ-	i	as in fight, night, right
ai	ใ-	i	as in drive, five, die
au	เ-า	ou	as in trout, count, shout
ia	เ-ียะ	ia	(short sound for 'ia')
ia	เ-ีย	ia	as in India, Australia, bier
oe	เ-อะ	-	(No English equivalent, but in German schön)
oe	เ-อ	-	(No English equivalent, but in German hören, nötig)
ua	วะ	ou	as in tour, pour
ua	ว	ou	as in sure, poor
uea	เ-อะ	-	(No English equivalent, but in
uea	เ-อ	-	German für, Tür, dafür)

To sum up, the vowels used in this book are as follows:

A   a, a, ae, ae, ai, au, am, aw, aw

E   e, e

I   i, i, ia, ia

O   o, <u>o</u>, oe, <u>oe</u>

U   u, <u>u</u>, ue, <u>ue</u>, ua, <u>ua</u>, uea, <u>uea</u>

Notes: 1. The line underneath indicates a long sound, no line means a short sound.

2. The line in Thai vowels indicates where the stem consonant of the word is placed.

5) **Word Units.** The Thai language has no punctuation, or capital or small letters. All words have fixed tones and exact pronunciations. However, in this text, the English capital letters are used to indicate the beginning of each word, and the hyphen (-) is used to separate the word units: Bòd, Tî-nùeng, Sà-wàd-di, etc.

5. แบบฝึกหัด / B<u>àe</u>b-fùeg-h<u>à</u>d / Exercises

1) Practice saying the following words:

ครับ	Krâb
ค่ะ	Kâ
คุณ	Kun
ขอบคุณ	K<u>à</u>wb-kun
โชคดี	Ch<u>ô</u>k-d<u>i</u>
ดิฉัน	Dì-chăn
สวัสดี	Sà-wàd-d<u>i</u>

2) Practice saying the following words and phrases:

พูด	P<u>û</u>d
พูดไทย	P<u>û</u>d-tai
พูดไทยได้	P<u>û</u>d-tai Dâi
พูดไทยได้ไหม	P<u>û</u>d-tai Dâi Măi
พูดไทยได้นิดหน่อย	P<u>û</u>d-tai Dâi Nîd-n<u>à</u>wy
ไทย	Tai

ประเทศไทย	Prà-têd-tai
เดินทาง	Doen-tang
หนังสือ	Năng-sŭe
หนังสือเดินทาง	Năng-sŭe-doen-tang
คน	Kon
ตรวจ	Trùad
ตรวจคน	Trùad-kon
เข้า	Kâo
เมือง	Mueang
เข้าเมือง	Kǎo-mueang
ตรวจคนเข้าเมือง	Trùad-kon-kao-mueang
ด่าน	Dàn
ด่านตรวจคนเข้าเมือง	Dàn Trùad-kon-kâo-mueang

2) Practice speaking the following sentences, and repeat until you can remember them.

(1) Sà-wàd-di Krâb

(2) Sà-wàd-di Kâ

(3) Kun Pûd Tai Dâi Mǎi Krâb

(4) Ka, Dì-chǎn Pûd Dâi Nîd-nàwy Kâ

(5) Kǎw T âwn-râb Sù Prà-têd-tai

(6) Kàwb-kun Mâg Kâ

(7) Kǎw Du Năng-sŭe-doen-tang

(8) Yù Tî-nî Kâ

(9) Kǎw Du T ǔa Krûeang-bin Dûay

(10) Kun Yù Mueang-tai Dâi Nùeng Duean

(11) Kun Jà Pâg Tî-nǎi

บทที่ 2	Bòd-Tî-sǎwng	Second Lesson
คุณพูดไทยได้	Kun Pûd Tai	Can You
ไหม	Dâi Mǎi?	Speak Thai?

1. บทสนทนา / Bòd Sǒn-tâ-na / Conversation

1) ก: คุณพูดไทยได้ไหม

Kun Pûd Tai Dâi Mǎi?

Can you speak Thai?

ข: พูดได้ ผมเป็นคนไทย

Pûd Dâi Pǒm Pen Kon-tai

(I) can speak (Thai). I am Thai.

2) ก: คุณพูดอังกฤษได้ไหม

Kun Pûd Ang-grìd Dâi Mǎi?

Can you speak English?

ข: ครับ พูดได้บ้าง

Krâb Pûd Dâi Bâng.

Yes, I can speak some.

3) ก: พาพวกเราไปที่นี่ได้ไหม

Pa Pûag-rao Pai Tî-nî Dâi Măi?

Can you take us to this place?

ข: อ๋อ ผมรู้จัก โรงแรมวินด์เซอร์

Ăw Pŏm Rú-jàg. Rong-raem Win-soe

I see. I know (it). Windsor Hotel.

4) ก: ราคาเท่าไร

Ra-ka Tâo-rai?

How much is the price?

ข: ผมคิดไม่แพง สองร้อยบาทเท่านั้น

Pŏm Kìd Mâi Paeng Săwng-ráwy Bàd Tâo-nán.

(My) charge (is) not expensive. Only two hundred baht.

5) ก: ตกลง พวกเราไปกับคุณ ขับช้า ๆ หน่อยนะ

Tòg-long Pûag-rao Pai Gàb Kun Kàb Chá-chá Nàwy Nâ.

All right, we (will) go with you. Drive slowly, please.

ข: ครับ แต่ขับช้ามากไม่ได้ รถติดมาก ต้องรีบไป

Krâb T àe Kàb Chá Mâg Mâi Dâi Râd Tìd Mâg T âwng Rîb Pai.

Yes, but (I) cannot drive very slowly. The traffic (will be) very heavy. (We) must hurry.

6) ก: ไม่เป็นไร ไม่ต้องรีบร้อน

Mâi Pen-rai Mâi-t âwng Rîb-ráwn.

Never mind. Don't hurry.

ข: ผมขับรถไม่เร็ว

Pǒm Kàb Rôd Mâi Rew.

I don't drive very fast.

7) ก: ผมไม่ชอบขับรถเร็วเหมือนกัน

Pǒm Mâi Ch<u>âw</u>b Kàb Rôd Rew M<u>ǔea</u>n-gan.

I don't like to drive fast, either.

ข: ถึงแล้ว

Tǔeng L<u>áe</u>w.

(We) have arrived.

2. คำศัพท์ / Kam-sàb / Vocabulary

คุณ	Kun	you
พูดไทย	P<u>û</u>d Tai	speak Thai, speaking Thai
ได้	Dâi	can
ไหม	Mǎi	question word, for yes/no answers
พูดได้	P<u>û</u>d Dâi	can speak
ผม	Pǒm	I (used by males)
เป็น	<u>P</u>en	am (is, are)
คนไทย	Kon Tai	Thai, Thai person, Thai people
พูดอังกฤษ	P<u>û</u>d Ang-grìd	speak English
อังกฤษ	Ang-grìd	English
บ้าง	B<u>â</u>ng	some
พา	P<u>a</u>	take
พาไป	P<u>a</u> Pai	take...to

เรา, พวกเรา	Rao, Pûag-rao	we, us
ที่นี่	Tî-nî	here
อ๋อ	Ăw	I see, exclamation for understanding
รู้จัก	Rú-jàg	know
วินด์เซอร์	Win-soe	Windsor
ราคา	Ra-ka	price, value
เท่าไร	Tâo-rai	How much
คิด	Kîd	charge
ไม่แพง	Mâi-paeng	inexpensive
สองร้อย	Săwng-ráwy	two hundred
บาท	Bàd	baht (Thai currency unit)
เท่านั้น	Tâo-nán	only
ตกลง	Tòg-long	all right, O.K.
กับ	Gàb	with
ขับ	Kàb	drive
ช้า ๆ	Chá-chá	slowly
หน่อยนะ	Nàwy-nâ	please
แต่	Tàe	but
ช้า	Chá	slow
มาก	Mâg	much
ไม่ได้	Mâi Dâi	cannot
รถติด	Rôd-tìd	heavy traffic
รถติดมาก	Rôd-tìd Mâg	very heavy traffic
ไม่ต้อง	Mâi-t âwng	don't, no need to
รีบร้อน	Rîb-ráwn	hurry

ไม่เป็นไร	Mâi Pen-rai	Nevermind,that'sO.K.
ไม่ต้องรีบร้อน	Mâi-t âwng Rîb-ráwn	Don't hurry
ถึง, มาถึง	Tŭeng, Ma-tŭeng	arrive
ถึงแล้ว	Tŭeng Láew	have arrived

3. หลักไวยากรณ์ / Làg Wai-ya-gawn / Grammar Points

1) ได้ Dâi = can, as in the following sentences:

   (1) ผมพูดไทยได้

      Pŏm Pûd Tai Dâi

      I can speak Thai.

   (2) คุณพูดไทยได้ไหม

      Kun Pûd Tai Dâi Măi?

      Can you speak Thai?

   (3) ผมพูดอังกฤษได้บ้าง

      Pŏm Pûd Ang-grìd Dâi Bâng

      I can speak some English.

2) ไหม Măi: question word for expecting yes/no answers, as in the following sentences:

   (1) คุณพูดไทยได้ไหม

      Kun Pûd Tai Dâi Măi?

      Can you speak Thai?

   (2) คุณพูดอังกฤษได้ไหม

      Kun Pûd Ang-grìd Dâi Măi?

      Can you speak English?

   (3) คุณพาพวกเราไปที่นี่ได้ไหม

      Kun Pa Pûag-rao Pai Tî-nî Dâi Măi?

      Can you take us to this place?

3) **ภาษาไทย** P<u>a</u>-s<u>ǎ</u> Tai = Thai language, **ภาษา** P<u>a</u>-s<u>ǎ</u> means 'language', put as a prefix to a word, as in the following examples:

ภาษาไทย	P<u>a</u>-s<u>ǎ</u> Tai	Thai language, Thai
ภาษาอังกฤษ	P<u>a</u>-s<u>ǎ</u> Ang-grìd	English language, English
ภาษาฝรั่งเศส	P<u>a</u>-s<u>ǎ</u> Fà-ràng-s<u>è</u>d	French language, French
ภาษาเยอรมัน	P<u>a</u>-s<u>ǎ</u> Y<u>oe</u>-râ-man	German language, German
ภาษาจีน	P<u>a</u>-s<u>ǎ</u> J<u>i</u>n	Chinese language, Chinese
ภาษาญี่ปุ่น	P<u>a</u>-s<u>ǎ</u> Yî-p<u>ù</u>n	Japanese language, Japanese

4) **คนไทย** Kon Tai = Thai people. '**คน**' ('Kon') means 'person', put as a prefix to a word to show nationality, as in the following examples:

คนไทย	Kon Tai	Thai person, Thai
คนจีน	Kon J<u>i</u>n	Chinese person, Chinese
คนญี่ปุ่น	Kon Yî-p<u>ù</u>n	Japanese person, Japanese
คนอังกฤษ	Kon Ang-grìd	Englishman, English
คนอเมริกัน	Kon A-m<u>e</u>-rî-gan	American
คนเยอรมัน	Kon Y<u>oe</u>-râ-man	German person, German
คนฝรั่งเศส	Kon Fà-ràng-s<u>è</u>d	Frenchman, French

คนคานาดา   Kon Ka-na-da   Canadian

คนออสเตรเลีย   Kon Áwd-sà-tre-lia   Australian

5) **ผม** Pŏm = I, me, used by males, as in the following sentences:

(1) **ผมเป็นคนไทย**

Pŏm Pen Kon Tai.

I am Thai.

(2) **ผมพูดไทยได้**

Pŏm Pûd Tai Dâi.

I can speak Thai.

(3) **ผมรู้จัก**

Pŏm Rú-jàg.

I know.

6) **หน่อยนะ** Nàwy-nâ. Here used at the end of a sentence as a request, to ask someone to do something a little bit less or more, as in the following examples: (Nǎwy = a little bit)

(1) **ขับช้า ๆ หน่อยนะ**

Kàb Chá-chá Nàwy-nâ.

Drive a little bit slowly please.

(2) **มาเร็ว ๆ หน่อยนะ**

Ma Rew-rew Nàwy-nâ

Come a little bit early please.

(3) **โชคดีนะ**

Chôk-di Nâ.

Good luck to you.

(4) **ขับช้า ๆ นะ**

Kàb Chá-chá Nâ.

Drive slowly please.

4. แบบฝึกหัด / B**à̲eb**-f**ùeg-h**à**d** / Excercises

1) Practice saying the following words:

คนไทย	Kon Tai	Thai person, Thai people
พูดไทย	P**û̲d** Tai	speak Thai
คนอังกฤษ	Kon Ang-gr**ì**d	Englishman
พูดอังกฤษ	P**û̲d** Ang-gr**ì**d	speak English
พวกเรา	P**û̲a̲g**-rao	we
เท่าไร	Tâo-rai	how much
ไม่แพง	Mâi-p**a̲e̲ng**	inexpensive
สองร้อย	S**ǎ̲w̲ng**-r**á̲w̲y**	two hundred
เท่านั้น	Tâo-nán	only
ตกลง	Tòg-long	O.K.
ช้า ๆ	Ch**á̲**-ch**á̲**	slowly
เร็ว ๆ	Rew-rew	quickly
หน่อยนะ	N**à̲w̲y**-nâ	a little bit... please
ไม่ได้	Mâi Dâi	cannot
ไม่ต้อง	Mâi-t **â̲w̲ng**	don't
ไม่เป็นไร	Mâi **P̲e̲n**-rai	never mind
รถติด	Rôd-t**ì̲d**	heavy traffic
รีบร้อน	R**î̲b**-r**á̲w̲n**	hurry
มาถึง	Ma**-**t**ǔ̲eng**	arrive
ถึงแล้ว	T**ǔ̲eng** L**á̲e̲w**	have arrived
มาถึงแล้ว	Ma**-**t**ǔ̲eng** L**á̲e̲w**	have arrived
ไม่ต้องรีบร้อน	Mâi-t **â̲w̲ng** R**î̲b**-r**á̲w̲n**	don't hurry

2) Practice saying the following words:

ไทย	Tai	Thai

ภาษาไทย	Pa-sǎ Tai	Thai language
จีน	Jin	Chinese
ภาษาจีน	Pa-sǎ Jin	Chinese language
ญี่ปุ่น	Yî-pùn	Japanese
ภาษาญี่ปุ่น	Pa-sǎ Yî-pùn	Japanese language
อังกฤษ	Ang-grìd	English
ภาษาอังกฤษ	Pa-sǎ Ang-grìd	English language
ฝรั่งเศส	Fà-ràng-sèd	French
ภาษาฝรั่งเศส	Pa-sǎ Fà-ràng-sèd	French language
เยอรมัน	Yoe-râ-man	German
ภาษาเยอรมัน	Pa-sǎ Yoe-râ-man	German language

3) Practice saying the following words:

ไทย	Tai	Thai
คนไทย	Kon Tai	Thai person
จีน	Jin	Chinese
คนจีน	Kon Jin	Chinese person
ญี่ปุ่น	Yî-pùn	Japanese
คนญี่ปุ่น	Kon Yî-pùn	Japanese person
อังกฤษ	Ang-grìd	English
คนอังกฤษ	Kon Ang-grìd	Englishman
ฝรั่งเศส	Fà-ràng-sèd	French
คนฝรั่งเศส	Kon Fà-ràng-sèd	Frenchman
เยอรมัน	Yoe-râ-man	German
คนเยอรมัน	Kon Yoe-râ-man	German person

4) Practice saying the following sentences:

(1) **คนไทยพูดไทย**　　　　Kon Tai Pûd Tai.

(2) **คนจีนพูดจีนได้**　　　　Kon Jin Pûd Jin Dâi.

(3) คนญี่ปุ่นพูดญี่ปุ่น   Kon Yî-pùn Pûd Yî-pùn.

(4) คนอังกฤษพูดอังกฤษ   Kon Ang-grìd Pûd Ang-grìd.

(5) คนฝรั่งเศสพูดฝรั่งเศส   Kon Fà-ràng-sèd Pûd Fà-ràng-sèd.

(6) คนเยอรมันพูดเยอรมัน   Kon Yoe-râ-man Pûd Yoe-râ-man.

5) Practice saying the following sentences:

(1) คนไทยพูดภาษาไทย   Kon Tai Pûd Pa-sǎ Tai.

(2) คนจีนพูดภาษาจีน   Kon Jin Pûd Pa-sǎ Jin.

(3) คนญี่ปุ่นพูดภาษาญี่ปุ่น   Kon Yî-pùn Pûd Pa-sǎ Yî-pùn.

(4) คนอังกฤษพูดภาษาอังกฤษ   Kon Ang-grìd Pûd Pa-sǎ Ang-grìd.

(5) คนฝรั่งเศสพูดภาษาฝรั่งเศส   Kon Fà-ràng-sèd Pûd Pa-sǎ Fa-rang-sèd.

(6) คนเยอรมันพูดภาษาเยอรมัน   Kon Yoe-râ-man Pûd Pa-sǎ Yoe-râ-man.

6) Practice saying the following sentences:

(1) ผมพูดภาษาไทยได้

Pom Pûd Tai Dâi.

(2) คนจีนพูดภาษาไทยได้

Kon Jin Pûd Pa-sǎ Tai Dâi.

(3) คนญี่ปุ่นพูดภาษาไทยได้

Kon Yî-pùn Pûd Pa-sǎ Tai Dâi.

(4) คนอังกฤษพูดภาษาฝรั่งเศสได้

Kon Ang-grìd Pûd Pa-sǎ Fà-ràng-sèd Dâi.

(5) คนเยอรมันพูดภาษาอังกฤษได้

Kon Yoe-râ-man Pûd Pa-sǎ Ang-grìd Dâi.

(6) พวกเราพูดภาษาไทยได้

Pûag-rao Pûd Pa-sǎ Tai Dâi.

(7) ผมพูดภาษาอังกฤษได้

Pǒm Pûd Pa-sǎ Ang-grìd Dâi.

(8) คุณพูดภาษาไทยได้

Kun Pûd Pa-sǎ Tai Dâi.

7) Practice saying the following sentences:

(1) Kun Pûd Tai Dâi Mǎi?

(2) Pûd Dâi. Pǒm Pen Kon Tai.

(3) Kun Pud Ang-grid Dai Mai?

(4) Pǒm Pûd Dâi Bâng.

(5) Kun Pa Pûag-rao Pai Tî-nî Dâi Mǎi.

(6) Pai Rong-raem Win-soe.

(7) Ra-ka Tâo-rai?

(8) Pǒm Kîd Mâi-paeng.

(9) Sǎwng-ráwy Bàd Tâo-nán.

(10) Tòg-long, Pûag-rao Pai Gàb Kun.

(11) Kàb Chá-chá Nàwy-nâ.

(12) Kàb Chá Mâg Mâi Dâi. Rôd-tìd Mâg.

(13) Mâi Pen-rai. Mâi-t âwng Rîb-ráwn.

(14) Pǒm Kàb Rôd Mâi Rew.

(15) Pǒm Mâi Châwb Kàb Rôd Rew Mǔean-gan.

(16) Tǔeng Láew.

| บทที่ 3 | Bòd Tî-sǎm | The Third Lesson |
| รอที่นี่ | R<u>aw</u> Tî-nî | Wait Here |

1. บทสนทนา / Bòd Sǒn-tâ-n<u>a</u> / Conversation

1) ก: ผมรอที่นี่

Pǒm R<u>aw</u> Tî-nî.

I (will) wait here.

ข: ไม่ต้องรอ วันนี้พวกเราไม่ไปไหนอีก

Mâi-t<u>ǎw</u>ng R<u>aw</u>. Wan-nî P<u>ûa</u>g-rao Mâi <u>P</u>ai Nǎi Ìg.

Don't wait. We won't go anywhere else today.

2) ก: คุณพักที่นี่หรือ

Kun Pâg Tî-nî R<u>ǔe</u>?

Do you stay here?

ข: ใช่ พวกเราพักที่โรงแรมนี้

Châi, Pûag-rao Pâg Tî Rong-raem Ní.

Yes, we stay at this hotel.

3) ก: คุณจะกลับเมื่อไร

Kun Jà Glàb Mûea-rai?

When will you leave?

ข: พวกเราจะกลับมะรืนนี้

Pûag-rao Jà Glàb Mâ-ruen-ní.

We will leave the day after tomorrow.

4) ก: พรุ่งนี้คุณจะไปไหน

Prûng-ni Kun Jà Pai Năi?

Where will you go tomorrow?

ข: จะไปซื้อของ

Jà Pai Súe-kăwng.

(We) will go shopping.

5) ก: คุณจะใช้รถแท๊กซี่ไหมครับ

Kun Jà Chái Rôd Táeg-sî Măi Krâb?

Will you use the taxi, sir?

ข: พวกเราจะใช้แท๊กซี่โรงแรม

Pûag-rao Jà Chái Táeg-sî Rong-raem.

We will use the hotel taxi.

6) ก: ผมจะช่วยขนกระเป๋า

Pŏm Jà Chûay Kŏn Grà-păo.

I will help (you) carry the luggage.

ข: ขอบคุณมาก

Kàwb-kun Mâg.

Thank you very much.

7) ก: พบกันใหม่นะครับ

Pôb-gan Mài Nâ Krâb.

See you again.

ข: **ครับพบกันใหม่พรุ่งนี้**

Krâb, Pôb-gan Mài Prûng-ní.

Yes, see you again tomorrow.

2. คำศัพท์ / Kam-sàb / Vocabulary

ที่นี่	Tî-nî	here, this place
รอ	Raw	wait
ไม่ต้อง	Mâi-t âwng	don't, no need to
วันนี้	Wan-ní	today
เรา	Rao	we
ไม่	Mâi	not, no
ไป	Pai	go
ไหน	Năi	anywhere
อีก	Ìg	else
พัก	Pâg	stay
หรือ	Rŭe	question word, expecting yes/no answers
ที่	Tî	at
ใช่	Châi	yes
โรงแรม	Rong-raem	hotel
นี้	Ní	this
จะ	Jà	will
กลับ	Glàb	leave, return
เมื่อไร	Mûea-rai	when

พรุ่งนี้	Prûng-ní	tomorrow
มะรืนนี้	Mâ-ruen-ní	the day after tomorrow
ซื้อของ	Súe-kǎwng	shopping
ใช้	Chái	use
แท๊กซี่	Táeg-sî	taxi
แท๊กซี่โรงแรม	Táeg-sî Rong-raem	hotel taxi
ช่วย	Chûay	help
ขน	Kǒn	carry
กระเป๋า	Grà-pǎo	luggage, bag
เดินทาง	Doen-tang	travel, traveling
กระเป๋าเดินทาง	Grà-pǎo-doen-tang	travel luggage
ขอบคุณ	Kàwb-kun	thank you, thanks
พบกัน	Pôb-gan	meet each other, see each other
ใหม่	Mài	again, new
พบกันใหม่	Pôb-gan Mài	See you again
พบกันอีก	Pôb-gan Ìg	See you again

3. หลักไวยากรณ์ / Làg Wai-ya-gawn / Grammar Points

1) จะ Jà; will, an auxiliary verb, used before a verb, as in the following sentences:

(1) คุณจะไปไหน

Kun Jà Pai Nǎi?

Where will you go?

(2) พรุ่งนี้คุณจะไปไหน

Prûng-ní Kun Jà Pai Nǎi?

Where will you go tomorrow?

(3) พวกเราจะไปซื้อของ

Pûag-rao Jà Pai Súe-kǎwng.

We will go shopping.

2) **ผม/ดิฉัน** Pǒm / Dì-chǎn: first person pronouns. Pǒm is used by males, and Dì-chǎn is used by females. Here are all of the Thai pronouns:

ผม	Pǒm	I, me (used by males)
ดิฉัน	Dì-chǎn	I, me (used by females)
คุณ	Kun	you, you (subject and object)
เขา	Kǎo	he, him, she, her
มัน	Man	it
พวกเรา	Pûag-rao	we, us
พวกคุณ	Pûag-kun	you, you (subject and object, plural)
พวกเขา	Pûag-kao	they, them

(1) **เขา** Kǎo: used to denote either gender, but may be accompained by particles to specify, as follows:

เขาผู้ชาย	Kǎo-pû-chay	he, him (... who is a man) (Pû-chay = man)
เขาผู้หญิง	Kǎo-pûu-yǐng	she, her (... who is a woman) (Pû-yǐng = woman)

(2) **พวกเรา** Pûag-rao: we (of a group) (Pûag = group, team)

เรา	Rao	we
เราทั้งหลาย	Rao-táng-lǎy	we (many of us)
		(Táng-lǎy = many)
(3)	พวกคุณ Pûag-kun:	you (of a group)
คุณ	Kun	you
พวกคุณ	Pûag-kun	you (many of you)
(4)	พวกเขา Pûag-kǎo:	they (of a group)
เขา	Kǎo	they
เขาทั้งหลาย	Kǎo-táng-lǎy	they (many of them)

4. แบบฝึกหัด / Bàeb-fùeg-hàd / Exercises

1) Practice saying the following words:

ไม่ต้อง	Mâi-tâwng	Don't
โรงแรม	Rong-raem	hotel
แท็กซี่	Tâeg-sî	taxi
ซื้อของ	Súe-kǎwng	shopping, buying things
กระเป๋า	Grà-pǎo	luggage, bag
ขอบคุณ	Kàwb-kun	thank you
วันนี้	Wan-ní	today
พรุ่งนี้	Prûng-ní	tomorrow
มะรืนนี้	Mâ-ruen-ní	the day after tomorrow

2) Practice saying the following words or phrases:

ขอบคุณ

Kàwb-kun   thank you

ขอบคุณมาก

Kàwb-kun Mâg ขอบคุณมากครับ	thank you very much
Kàwb-kun Mâg Krâb กระเป๋า	thank you very much, sir
Grà-pǎo เดินทาง	luggage
Doen-tang กระเป๋าเดินทาง	travel
Grà-pǎo-doen-tang พบกัน	travel luggage
Pôb-gan. พบกันใหม่	See you.
Pôb-gan Mài. พบกันใหม่นะ	See you again.
Pôb-gan Mài Nâ. พบกันใหม่นะครับ	See you again (please).
Pôb-gan Mài Nâ Krâb. พบกันใหม่พรุ่งนี้	See you again (please, sir).
Pôb-gan Mài Prûng-nì. พบกันใหม่พรุ่งนี้นะครับ	See you again tomorrow.
Pôb-gan Mài Prûng-ní Nâ Krâb.	See you again tomorrow (please, sir).

3) Practice saying the following sentences:

(1) ผมจะไปซื้อของ

Pǒm Jà Pai Súe-kǎwng.   I will go shopping.

(2) ดิฉันจะไปซื้อของ

Di-chǎn Jà Pai Súe-kǎwng.   I will go shopping.

(3) เขาจะไปซื้อของ

Kao Jà Pai Súe-kǎwng.   He (She) will go shopping.

(4) พวกเราจะไปซื้อของ

Pûag-rao Jà Pai Súe-kǎwng. We will go shopping.

(5) พวกคุณจะไปซื้อของ

Pûag-kun Jà Pai Súe-kǎwng. You will go shopping.

(6) พวกเราจะไปซื้อของ

Pûag-rao Jà Pai Súe-kǎwng. We will go shopping.

4) Practice saying the following sentences:

(1) ผมพักที่นี่

Pǒm Pâg Tî-nî.   I stay here.

(2) คุณพักที่นี่

Kun Pâg Tî-nî.   You stay here.

(3) เขาผู้ชายพักที่นี่

Kǎo Pû-chay Pâg Tî-nî.   He stays here.

(4) เขาผู้หญิงพักที่นี่

Kǎo Pû-yǐng Pâg Tî-nî.   She stays here.

(5) พวกเราพักที่นี่

Pûag-rao Pâg Tî-nî.   We stay here.

(6) พวกคุณพักที่นี่

Pûag-kun Pâg Tî-nî.   You stay here.

(7) พวกเขาพักที่นี่

Pûag-kao Pâg tî-nî.   They stay here.

5) Practice saying the following sentences:

(1) คุณจะพักที่นี่หรือ

Kun Jà Pâg Tî-nî Rǔe?   Will you stay here?

(2) เขาจะพักที่นี่หรือ

Kǎo Jà Pâg Tî-nî Rǔe?   Will he/she stay here?

(3) เขาผู้ชายจะพักที่นี่หรือ

Kǎo Pû-ch<u>ay</u> Jà Pâg Tî-nî   Will he stay here?

R<u>ǔe</u>?

(4) เขาผู้หญิงจะพักที่นี่หรือ

Kǎo Pû-yǐng Jà Pâg Tî-nî   Will she stay here?

R<u>ǔe</u>?

(5) พวกเราจะพักที่นี่หรือ

P<u>û</u>ag-rao Jà Pâg Tî-nî Rǔe?   Will we stay here?

(6) พวกคุณจะพักที่นี่หรือ

P<u>û</u>ag-kun Jà Pâg Tî-nî Rǔe?   Will you stay here?

(7) พวกเขาจะพักที่นี่หรือ

P<u>û</u>ag-kǎo Jà Pag Tî-nî Rǔe?   Will they stay here?

6) Practice saying the following sentences:

(1) Pǒm R<u>aw</u> Tî-nî.

(2) Mâi-tâ<u>w</u>ng R<u>aw</u>.

(3) Kun Pâg Tî R<u>o</u>ng-raem Ní Rǔe?

(4) Châi, P<u>û</u>ag-rao Pâg Tî R<u>o</u>ng-r<u>ae</u>m Ní.

(5) Kun Jà Glàb M<u>û</u>ea-rai?

(6) P<u>û</u>ag-rao Jà Glàb Mâ-r<u>ue</u>n-ní.

(7) Kun Jà Chái T<u>á</u>eg-s<u>i</u> Mai Krab?

(8) Jà Chái T<u>á</u>eg-sî R<u>o</u>ng-r<u>ae</u>m.

(9) P<u>û</u>ag-kun Jà P<u>a</u>i Nǎi?

(10) P<u>û</u>ag-rao Jà P<u>a</u>i Súe-kǎ<u>w</u>ng.

(11) Pǒm Jà Ch<u>û</u>ay Kun Kǒn Grà-pǎo-d<u>oe</u>n-t<u>a</u>ng.

บทที่ 4   Bòd Tî-sî   The Fourth Lesson

กินอาหารไทย   Gin A-hǎn Tai   Eat Thai Food

1. บทสนทนา / Bòd Sǒn-tâ-na / Conversation

1) ก: พวกเราต้องการไปกินอาหารไทย คุณจะแนะนำสถาน
ที่ได้ไหมครับ

Pûag-rao Tâwng-gan Pai Gin A-hǎn Tai. Kun Jà Nâe-
nam Sà-tǎn-tî Dâi Mǎi Krâb?

We want to go eat Thai food. Could you recommend a
place?

ข: ผมจะพาคุณไปร้านอาหารใหญ่ที่สุดในโลก

Pǒm Jà Pa Kun Pai Rán-a-hǎn Yài Tî-sùd Nai Lôg.

I will take you to the biggest restaurant in the world.

2) ก: จริง ๆ หรือ อยู่ที่ไหน

Jing-jing Rŭe? Yù Tî-nǎi?

Really? Where is it?

ข: อยู่ไม่ไกลจากที่นี่

Yŭ Mâi Glai Jàg Tî-nî.

(It) is not far from here.

3) ก: พวกเราจะไปเมื่อไร

Pûag-rao Jà Pai Mûea-rai?

When will we go?

ข: ไปทันทีเลย ใกล้ถึงหนึ่งทุ่มแล้ว

Pai Tan-ti Loey. Glâi-tŭeng Nùeng Tûm Láew.

(We'll) go right away. (It's) almost seven PM already.

4) ก: เราเดินหรือไปแท๊กซี่

Rao Doen Rŭe Pai Tâeg-sî?

Do we walk or go by taxi?

ข: ไปแท๊กซี่ดีกว่า ถึงแล้ว คุณดูซิมันใหญ่ไหม

Pai Táeg-sî Di-gwà. Tŭeng Láew. Kun Du Sî Man Yài Mǎi.

We'd better go by taxi. (We've) arrived. You have a look whether it's big.

5) ก: ใหญ่มากจริง ๆ มีคนกินอยู่ที่นี่มากเท่าไร

Yài Mâg Jing-jing. Mi Kon Gin Yù Tî-nî Mâg Tâo-rai.

(It's) really big. How many people are eating here?

ข: รับรองแขกเวลาเดียวกันได้ประมาณสามพันคน

Râb-rawng Kàeg We-la Diaw-gan Dâi Prà-man Sǎm-pan Kon.

(It) can entertain about 3,000 guests at the same time.

6) ก: เขาขายอาหารไทยเท่านั้นหรือ

Kǎo Kǎy A-hǎn Tai Tâo-nán Rǔe?

Do they sell only Thai food?

ข: ไม่ครับ มีอาหารไทย อาหารจีน อาหารญี่ปุ่น และ อาหารฝรั่ง แต่อาหารไทยเป็นที่นิยมมากที่สุด

Mâi Krâb, Mi A-hǎn Tai A-hǎn Jin A-hǎn Yî-pùn Lâe A-hǎn Fà-ràng. T àe A-hǎn Tai Pen-tî-nî-yom Mâg Tî-sùd.

No sir, there are Thai food, Chinese food, Japanese food and European food. But Thai food is the most popular.

7) ก: มีรำไทยด้วยไหม พวกเราอยากดูรำไทย

Mi Ram-tai Dûay Mǎi? Pûag-rao Yàg Du Ram-tai.

Is there also Thai classical dancing? We want to see Thai dancing.

ข: ครับ มีรำไทยด้วย เขาเริ่มแสดงเวลาประมาณสองทุ่ม

Krâb, Mi Ram-tai Dûay. Kǎo Rôem Sà-daeng We-la Prà-man Sǎwng Tûm.

Yes, there's Thai dancing, too. They start the show at about eight PM.

2. คำศัพท์ / Kam-sàb / Vocabulary

เรา พวกเรา	Rao, Pûag-rao	we
ต้องการ	T âwng-gan	want, would like
กิน	Gin	eat
อาหาร	A-hǎn	food
อาหารไทย	A-hǎn Tai	Thai food
คุณ	Kun	you
จะ	Jà	will

แนะนำ	Nâe-nam	recommend
สถานที่	Sà-tǎn-tî	place
ได้	Dâi	can
ไหม	Mǎi	question word, expecting yes/no answers
ผม	Pǒm	I
พา	Pa	take
ร้าน	Rán	shop; store
ร้านอาหาร	Rán-a-hǎn	food shop, restaurant
ใหญ่	Yài	big
ใหญ่ที่สุด	Yài Tî-sùd	the biggest
จริง ๆ	Jing-jing	really
หรือ	Rǔe	question word, expecting yes/no answers
อยู่	Yù	is (am, are, etc)
ที่ไหน	Tî-nǎi	where
ไม่	Mâi	not
ไกล	Glai	far
ไม่ไกล	Mâi Glai	not far
จาก	Jàg	from
ที่นี่	Tî-nî	here, this place
เมื่อไร	Mûea-rai	when
ทันที	Tan-ti	right away, immediately

เลย	Loey	go ahead, ending particle to show agreement of the speaker
ใกล้	Glâi	near, almost
ถึง	Tŭeng	to
หนึ่งทุ่ม	Nùeng Tûm	seven PM, seven o'clock in the evening
แล้ว	Láew	already
เดิน	Doen	walk
ไป	Pai	go
แท๊กซี่	Táeg-sî	taxi
ดีกว่า	Di-gwà	better
ถึง	Tŭeng	arrive
ถึงแล้ว	Tŭeng Láew	have arrived
ดู	Du	see, have a look
ซิ	Sî	please, ending particle for a request or an order
ดูซิ	Du Sî	please have a look
มัน	Man	it
ใหญ่	Yài	big
ใหญ่มาก	Yài Mâg	very big
จริง ๆ	Jing-jing	really, indeed
คน	Kon	person, people
มาก	Mâg	many

มากเท่าไร	Mâg Tâo-rai	how many
รับรอง	Râb-rawng	entertain
แขก	Kàeg	guest
เวลา	We-la	time
เดียวกัน	Diaw-gan	the same
เวลาเดียวกัน	We-la Diaw-gan	at the same time
ได้	Dâi	can
ประมาณ	Prà-man	about, approximately
สามพัน	Sǎm-pan	three thousand
ขาย	Kǎy	sell
เท่านั้น	Tâo-nán	only
จีน	Jin	Chinese
อาหารจีน	A-hǎn Jin	Chinese food
ญี่ปุ่น	Yî-pùn	Japanese
อาหารญี่ปุ่น	A-hǎn Yî-pùn	Japanese food
ฝรั่ง	Fà-ràng	European
อาหารฝรั่ง	A-hǎn Fà-ràng	European food
แต่	Tàe	but
เป็นที่นิยม	Pen-tî-nî-yom	popular
มากที่สุด	Mâg Tî-sùd	the most
รำ	Ram	dancing
รำไทย	Ram-tai	Thai dancing
ด้วย	Dûay	too, as well, also
เริ่ม	Rôem	start
แสดง	Sà-daeng	show, showing
สองทุ่ม	Sǎwng Tûm	eight PM, eight o'clock in the evening

3. หลักไวยากรณ์ / Làg Wai-ya-gawn / Grammar Points

1) แล้ว Láew = already, then ; used in the present perfect tense, as in the following examples (please note how to use 'then' in Examples 4 and 5):

(1) **พวกเรามาถึงแล้ว**

Pûag-rao Ma-tŭeng Láew.

We have arrived. We have already arrived.

(2) **ผมกินแล้ว**

Pŏm Gin Láew.

I have already eaten. I have eaten.

(3) **แท๊กซี่ไปแล้ว**

Táeg-sî Pai Láew.

The taxi has gone.

(4) **แล้วคุณจะไปไหน**

Láew Kun Jà Pai Năi?

Then, where will you go?

(5) **แล้วเขาจะมาอีกไหม**

Láew Kăo Jà Ma Ìg Măi?

Then, will he come again?

2) เลย Loey = go ahead, a particle used as an adverb for a request or an order/command, as in the following examples:

(1) **กินเลย**

Gin Loey!   Eat! Go ahead (and) eat!

(2) **ไปเลย**

Pai Loey!   Go! Go away! Go ahead!

(3) **เข้ามาเลย**

Kâo-ma Loey!   Please enter! Come in!

3) ซิ Sî = please, go ahead; here a particle used as an adverb at the end of a sentence as a request or command, similar to 'L<u>oe</u>y'.

(1) กินซิ

    Gin Sî!   Eat! Please eat!

(2) ไปซิ

    <u>P</u>ai Sî!   Go! Please go!

(3) เข้ามาซิ

    Kâo-m<u>a</u> Sî!   Enter! Please enter!

4) เวลา W<u>e</u>-l<u>a</u> = time; in spoken language, Thai people tell the time as follows:

1 ทุ่ม	Nùeng Tûm	7 PM
2 ทุ่ม	S<u>ǎw</u>ng Tûm	8 PM
3 ทุ่ม	S<u>ǎ</u>m Tûm	9 PM
4 ทุ่ม	Sì Tûm	10 PM
5 ทุ่ม	H<u>â</u> Tûm	11 PM
6 ทุ่ม	Hòg Tûm	12 AM
ตี 1	T i Nueng	1 AM
ตี 2	T i S<u>ǎw</u>ng	2 AM
ตี 3	T i S<u>ǎ</u>m	3 AM
ตี 4	T i Sì	4 AM
ตี 5	T i H<u>â</u>	5 AM
6 โมงเช้า	Hòg M<u>o</u>ng Cháo	6 AM
7 โมงเช้า	Jèd M<u>o</u>ng Cháo	7 AM
8 โมงเช้า	Pàed M<u>o</u>ng Cháo	8 AM
9 โมงเช้า	Gâo M<u>o</u>ng Cháo	9 AM
10 โมงเช้า	Sìb M<u>o</u>ng Cháo	10 AM
11 โมงเช้า	Sìb-èd M<u>o</u>ng Cháo	11 AM

12 โมง	Sìb-săwng Mong	12 PM
เที่ยง เที่ยงวัน	Tîang, Tîang-wan	
บ่ายโมง บ่าย 1 โมง	Bày (Nùeng) Mong	1 PM
บ่าย 2 (โมง)	Bày Săwng (Mong)	2 PM
บ่าย 3 (โมง)	Bày Săm (Mong)	3 PM
บ่าย 4 (โมง)	Bày Sì (Mong)	4 PM
บ่าย 5 (โมง)	Bày Hâ (Mong)	5 PM
5 โมงเย็น	Hâ Mong Yen	
6 โมงเย็น	Hòg Mong Yen	6 PM

Note: Words in brackets can be omitted. In written language, or as standard time, we tell the time as follows:

1 นาฬิกา	Nùeng Na-lî-ga	0100 hour, 1 o'clock
2 นาฬิกา	Săwng Na-lî-ga	0200 hours, 2 o'clock
3 นาฬิกา	Săm Na-lî-ga	0300 hours, 3 o'clock
6 นาฬิกา	Hòg Na-lî-ga	0600 hours, 6 o'clock
8 นาฬิกา	P àed Na-lî-ga	0800 hours, 8 o'clock
10 นาฬิกา	Sìb Na-lî-ga	1000 hours, 10 o'clock
15 นาฬิกา	Sìb-hâ Na-lî-ga	1500 hours, 3 o'clock

18 นาฬิกา	Sìb-p àed Na-lî-ga	1800 hours, 6 o'clock in the evening
24 นาฬิกา	Yî-sìb-sì Na-lî-ga	2400 hours, 12 o'clock in the evening

Note: In telling portions of the time, we say as follows:

ตีหนึ่งครึ่ง	Ti Nuèng Krûeng	1:30 AM
ตีสามครึ่ง	Ti Sǎm Krǔeng	3:30 AM
ตีสี่ครึ่ง	Ti Sì Krûeng	4:30 AM
หกโมงครึ่ง	Hòg Mong Krûeng	6:30 AM
สิบโมงยี่สิบ	Sìb Mong Yî-sìb	10:20 AM
สิบเอ็ดโมงสิบห้า	Sìb-èd Mong Sìb-hâ	11:15 AM
เที่ยงครึ่ง	Tîang Krûeng	12:30 PM
บ่ายสามโมงสิบห้า	Bày Sǎm Mong Sìb-hâ	3:15 PM
บ่ายสามโมงครึ่ง	Bày Sǎm Mong Krûeng	3:30 PM
บ่ายสามโมงสี่สิบห้า	Bày Sǎm Mong Sì-sìb-hâ	3:45 PM
บ่ายสามโมงห้าสิบ	Bày Sǎm Mong Hâ-sìb	3:50 PM
สองทุ่มครึ่ง	Sǎwng Tûm Krûeng	8:30 PM
สามทุ่มยี่สิบ	Sǎm Tûm Yî-sìb	9:20 PM

สิบห้านาฬิกา	Sìb-hâ Na-lî-ga	1530 hours
สามสิบนาที	Săm-sìb Na-ti	
สิบห้านาฬิกา	Sìb-hâ Na-lî-ga	1545 hours
สี่สิบห้านาที	Sì-sìb-hâ Na-ti	

Note: Some words for time expressions are as follows:

ชั่วโมง	Chûa-mong	hour
นาที	Na-ti	minute
วินาที	Wî-na-ti	second
ครึ่ง	Krûeng	half
กลางวัน	Glang-wan	daytime
กลางคืน	Glang-kuen	night-time
ดึก	Dùeg	late at night
สาย	Săy	late in the morning, behind schedule
เช้า	Cháo	morning
บ่าย	Bày	afternoon
สว่าง	Sà-wàng	bright, daylight
มืด	Mûed	dark, after sunset
ค่ำ	Kâm	dark, late afternoon
คืน	Kuen	night
วัน	Wan	day
นาฬิกา	Na-lî-ga	watch, clock, o'clock, hour

4. แบบฝึกหัด / Bàeb-fùeg-hàd / Exercises

1) Practice saying the following words:

| ไทย | Tai | Thai |

อาหาร	A-hǎn	food
อาหารไทย	A-hǎn Tai	Thai food
ร้านอาหารไทย	Rán-a-hǎn Tai	Thai restaurant
จีน	Jin	Chinese
อาหารจีน	A-hǎn Jin	Chinese food
ร้านอาหารจีน	Rán-a-hǎn Jin	Chinese restaurant
ญี่ปุ่น	Yî-pùn	Japanese
อาหารญี่ปุ่น	A-hǎn Yî-pùn	Japanese food
ร้านอาหารญี่ปุ่น	Rán-a-hǎn Yî-pùn	Japanese restaurant
ฝรั่ง	Fà-ràng	European
อาหารฝรั่ง	A-hǎn Fà-ràng	European food
ร้านอาหารฝรั่ง	Rán-a-hǎn Fà-ràng	European restaurant
ทะเล	Tâ-le	sea
อาหารทะเล	A-hǎn Tâ-le	seafood
ร้านอาหารทะเล	Rán-a-hǎn Tâ-le	seafood restaurant

2) Practice saying the following words and phrases:

หนึ่งทุ่ม	Nùeng Tûm	7 PM
บ่ายโมง	Bày Mong	1 PM
ตีห้า	T i Hâ	5 AM
เวลา	We-la	time
เดียวกัน	Diaw-gan	the same
เวลากลางวัน	We-la Glang-wan	daytime
เวลากลางคืน	We-la Glang-kuen	night-time

45

เที่ยงวัน	Tîang-wan	noon, 12 o'clock
เที่ยงคืน	Tîang-kuen	midnight, 12 AM
มืดค่ำ	Mûed-kâm	dark night
ดึกมากแล้ว	Dùeg Mâg Láew	very late at night already
สายแล้ว	Sǎy Láew	late in the morning already
เวลาทำงาน	We-la Tam-ngan	office hours, working time
เวลานอน	We-la Nawn	sleeping time
เวลากิน	We-la Gin	eating time
เวลาเดียวกัน	We-la Diaw-gan	(at) the same time
ทุกวัน	Tûg-wan	daily, every day
ทุกคืน	Tûg-kuen	nightly, every night

3) Practice saying the following sentences:

(1) เข้ามาเลย   Kâo-ma Loey!

(2) เชิญเลย   Choen Loey!

(3) เชิญกินได้เลย   Choen Gin Dâi Loey!

(4) นั่งลงซิ   Nâng long Sî!

(5) มาทางนี้ซิ   Ma Tang Ní Sî!

(6) บอกเขาซิ   Bàwg Kǎo Sî!

(7) ดูนี้ซิ   Du Ní Sî!

(8) สองชั่วโมงเท่านั้น   Sǎwng Chûa-mong Tâo-nán.

(9) ใกล้ถึงเวลาแล้ว   Glâi Tǔeng We-la Láew.

(10) มาเวลาเดียวกัน   Ma We-la Diaw-gan.

4) Practice saying the following time expressions in Thai:

1 PM   Bày Mong

2 PM	Bày Sǎwng Mọng
3 PM	Bày Sǎm Mọng
6 PM	Hòg Mọng Yen
9 PM	Sǎm Tûm
11 PM	Hậ Tûm
12 AM	Tîang-kuen, Hòg Tûm

5) Practice saying the following time expressions:

1 AM	Ti Nùeng
2 AM	Ti Sǎwng
3 AM	Ti Sǎm
6 AM	Hòg Mọng Cháo
9 AM	Gâo Mọng Cháo
10 AM	Sìb Mọng Cháo
11 AM	Sìb-èd Mọng Cháo
12 PM	Tîang-wan, Sìb-sǎwng Mọng

6) Practice saying the following time expressions:

1 PM	Bày Mọng
4 PM	Bày Sì (Mọng)
5 PM	Hậ Mọng Yen
7 PM	Nùeng Tûm
8 PM	Sǎwng Tûm
9 PM	Sǎm Tûm
10 PM	Sì Tûm
12 PM	Tîang-kuen

7) Practice saying the following time expressions:

0830 hours	Pàed Na-lî-ga Sǎm-sìb Na-ti

1000 hours	Sìb Na-lî-ga
1030 hours	Sìb Na-lî-ga Sǎm-sìb Na-ti
1145 hours	Sìb-èd Na-lî-ga
1630 hours	Sìb-hòg Na-lî-ga
2000 hours	Yî-sìb Na-lî-ga
2300 hours	Yî-sìb-sǎm Na-lî-ga
2445 hours	Yî-sìb-sì Na-lî-ga Sì-sìb-hâ Na-ti

8) Practice saying the following sentences:

(1) Rao T âwng-gan Pai Gin A-hǎn Tai.

(2) Kun Jà Nâe-nam Sà-tǎn-tî Dâi Mǎi?

(3) Pǒm Jà Pa Kun Pai Rán-a-hǎn Yài Tî-sùd Nai Lôg.

(4) Pûag-rao Jà Pai Mûea-rai?

(5) Pai Tan-ti Loey.

(6) Glâi Tǔeng Nùeng Tûm Láew.

(7) Rao Doen Rǔe Pai Tâeg-sî?

(8) Pai Táeg-sî Di-gwà.

(9) Kun Du Sî Man Yài Mǎi!

(10) Yài Mâg Jing-jing.

(11) Mi Kon Gin Yù Tî-nî Mâg Tâo-rai?

(12) Râb-rawng Kàeg We-la Diaw-gan Dâi Prà-man Sǎm-pan Kon.

(13) A-hǎn Tai Pen-tî-nî-yom Tî-sùd.

(14) Mi Ram-tai Dûay Mǎi?

(15) Pûag-rao Yàg Du Ram-tai.

(16) Kǎo Rôem Sà-daeng We-la Prà-man Sǎwng Tûm.

บทที่ 5	Bòd Tî-hâ	The Fifth Lesson
ผลไม้ไทย	Pǒn-lâ-mái Tai	Thai Fruit

1. บทสนทนา / Bòd Sǒn-tâ-na / Conversation

1) ก: คุณสนใจผลไม้บ้างไหมครับ

Kun Sǒn-jai Pǒn-lâ-mái Bâng Mǎi Krâb?

Are you interested in any fruit?

ข: ไม่ค่ะ ดิฉันไม่ชอบผลไม้มากนัก

Mâi Kâ, Dì-chǎn Mâi Châwb Pǒn-lâ-mái Mâg Nâg.

No, thanks. I don't like fruit very much.

2) ก: คุณไม่ลองผลไม้ไทยบ้างหรือ

Kun Mâi Lawng Pǒn-lâ-mái Tai Bâng Rǔe?

Don't you (want to) try some Thai fruit?

ข: ผลไม้ชนิดไหนค่ะ

Pŏn-lâ-mái Châ-nid Năi Kâ?

What kind of fruit?

3) ก: มีผลไม้หลายชนิดในฤดูนี้

Mi Pŏn-lâ-mai Lăy Châ-nid Nai Rûe-du Ní.

There are many kinds of fruit in this season.

ข: ดูซินั่น ผลไม้มีหนามนั้นคืออะไร

Du Sî Nân! Pŏn-lâ-mái Mi-năm Nan Kue À-rai?

Please look at that! What is that spiny fruit?

4) ก: (มันคือ) ทุเรียน

(Man Kue) Tû-rian.

(It is) durian.

ข: (มัน) มีกลิ่นเหม็นที่สุด

(Man) Mi-glín Měn Tî-sùd.

(It) smells the worst.

5) ก: ถ้าคุณชิมคุณจะชอบ มันเป็นผลไม้อร่อยที่สุด

Tâ Kun Chim Kun Jà Châwb. Man Pen Pŏn-lâ-mâi A-ràwy Tî-sùd.

If you taste (it), you will like (it). It's the most delicious (of fruit).

ข: ผลไม้อะไรอยู่ข้างทุเรียนนั้น

Pŏn-lâ-mai À-rai Yù Kâng Tû-rian?

What fruit is beside (the) durian?

6) ก: นั่นคือขนุน และใกล้ๆ ขนุนเป็นมังคุด

Nán Kue Kà-nŭn. Lâe Glâi-glâi Kà-nŭn Pen Mang-Kûd.

That's jackfruit. And near (the) jackfruit (there) are mangosteens.

ข: ดิฉันอยากลองชิมขนุน ชื่อแปลกดี

Dì-chǎn Yàg Lawng Chim Kà-nǔn. Chûe Plàeg Di.

I'd like to try to taste jackfruit. The name's quite strange.

7) ก: ลองทั้งหมดก็ได้ ทั้งขนุน มังคุด และทุเรียน คนไทย
ชอบรับประทานมังคุดหลังทุเรียน

Lawng Táng-mòd Gâw Dai. Táng Kà-nǔn, Mang-kûd,
Lâe Tû-rian. Kon Tai Châwb Râb-prà-tan Mang-kud Lǎng
Tû-rian.

(You can) try all of them. All jackfruit, mangosteen, and
durian. Thai people like to have mangosteen after durian.

ข: ไม่ค่ะ ยกเว้นทุเรียน ดิฉันยังไม่ชอบกลิ่นของมัน และ
ทนมันไม่ได้

Mâi Ka, Yôg-wén Tû-rian. Dì-chǎn Yang Mâi Châwb Glìn
Kǎwng-man, Lâe Ton Man Mâi Dâi.

No, thanks. (I'll try all of them) except durian. I still don't
like its smell, and can't bear it.

2. คำศัพท์ / Kam-sàb / Vocabulary

ผลไม้	Pǒn-lâ-mái	fruit
ผลไม้ไทย	Pǒn-lâ-mái Tai	Thai fruit
สนใจ	Sǒn-jai	interested
บ้าง	Bâng	any, some
ไม่	Mâi	no, not
ชอบ	Châwb	like
ไม่ชอบ	Mâi Châwb	not like
มาก	Mâg	much
มากนัก	Mâg Nâg	very much

ลอง	Lawng	try
ชนิด	Châ-nîd	kind
ชนิดไหน	Châ-nîd Nǎi	what kind....
หลาย	Lǎy	many
ใน	Nai	in
ฤดู	Rûe-du	season
นี้	Ní	this
ดู	Du	look, have a look
นั้น	Nân	that
ดูซินั่น	Du Sî Nân	have a look at that
หนาม	Nǎm	spine, thorn
มีหนาม	Mi-nǎm	spiny
คือ	Kue	is
อะไร	À-rai	what
ทุเรียน	Tû-rian	durian
กลิ่น	Glìn	smell
มีกลิ่น	Mi-glìn	(it) smells
เหม็น	Měn	bad smell, smelly
ที่สุด	Tî-sùd	the most
เหม็นที่สุด	Měn Tî-sùd	(it) smells the worst
ชิม	Chim	taste
อร่อย	À-ràwy	delicious
อร่อยที่สุด	À-ràwy Tî-sùd	most delicious
ข้าง	Kâng	beside
ขนุน	Kà-nǔn	jackfruit
ใกล้ๆ	Glâi-glâi	near
เป็น	Pen	is

มังคุด	Mang-kûd	mangosteen
ชื่อ	Chûe	name
แปลก	Plàeg	strange
ดี	Di	good, well
แปลกดี	Plàeg Di	quite strange
ทั้งหมด	Táng-mòd	all of them
ทั้ง	Táng	all
รับประทาน	Râb-prà-tan	have (eat)
หลัง, หลังจาก	Lăng, Lăng-jàg	after
ยกเว้น	Yôg-wén	except
ของมัน	Kăwng-man	its
มัน	Man	it
ทน	Ton	bear
ทนไม่ได้	Ton Mâi Dâi	can't bear

3. หลักไวยากรณ์ / Làg Wai-ya-gawn / Grammar Points

1) มัน Man = it: used as a subject or object. In Thai, spoken or written, we are likely to skip this word. It's considered impolite.

(1) มันคือทุเรียน

Man Kue Tû-rian.

It is durian.

(2) มันมีกลิ่นเหม็นมาก

Man Mi-glìn Měn Mâg.

It smells very bad.

(3) ถ้าคุณชิม (มัน) คุณจะชอบ (มัน)

Ta Kun Chim (Man), Kun Jà Châwb (Man).

If you taste it, you will like it.

2) ที่สุด Tî-sùd = the most, used in comparisons of adjectives and adverbs, 'Tî-sùd' for the superlative degree, and 'Gwà' for the comparative degree.

ดี	ดีกว่า	ดีที่สุด
Di	Di-gwà	Di-tî-sùd
good	better	best
แพง	แพงกว่า	แพงที่สุด
Paeng	Paeng-gwà	Paeng-tî-sùd
expensive	more expensive	most expensive
ถูก	ถูกกว่า	ถูกที่สุด
Tùg	Tùg-gwà	Tùg-tî-sùd
cheap	cheaper	cheapest
สวย	สวยกว่า	สวยที่สุด
Sǔay	Sǔay-gwà	Sǔay-tî-sùd
beautiful	more beautiful	most beautiful
เหม็น	เหม็นกว่า	เหม็นที่สุด
Měn	Měn-gwà	Měn-tî-sùd
smelly	smellier	smelliest
หนาว	หนาวกว่า	หนาวที่สุด
Nǎw	Nǎw-gwà	Nǎw-tî-sùd
cold	colder	coldest
ร้อน	ร้อนกว่า	ร้อนที่สุด
Ráwn	Ráwn-gwà	Ráwn-tî-sùd
hot	hotter	hottest

3) ที่ Tî, added to cardinal numbers to make them ordinal numbers.

ที่ 1   Tî-nùeng   the first

ที่ 2	Tî-sǎwng	the second
ที่ 3	Tî-sǎm	the third
ที่ 4	Tî-sì	the fourth
ที่ 5	Tî-hâ	the fifth
ที่ 6	Tî-hòg	the sixth
ที่ 7	Tî-jèd	the seventh
ที่ 8	Tî-p àed	the eighth
ที่ 9	Tî-gâo	the ninth
ที่ 10	Tî-sìb	the tenth
ที่ 11	Tî-sìb-èd	the eleventh
ที่ 12	Tî-sìb-sǎwng	the twelfth
ที่ 13	Tî-sìb-sǎm	the thirteenth
ที่ 15	Tî-sìb-hâ	the fifteenth
ที่ 20	Tî-yî-sìb	the twentieth
ที่ 25	Tî-yî-sìb-hâ	the twenty fifth
ที่ 28	Tî-yî-sìb-p àed	the twenty-eighth
ที่ 30	Tî-sǎm-sìb	the thirtieth
ที่ 31	Tî-sǎm-sìb-èd	the thirty-first

4. แบบฝึกหัด / Bàeb-fùeg-hàd / Exercises

1) Practice saying the following words:

ทำไม	Tam-mai	why
ไม่ได้	Mâi Dâi	cannot
ผลไม้	Pǒn-lâ-mái	fruit
ดีไหม	Di Mǎi	Is it good?
ไม่ดี	Mâi di	not good
ไม่ชอบ	Mâi Châwb	do not like

ชนิดไหน	Châ-nîd Năi	what kind...
สนใจ	Sŏn-jai	interested
ลองชิม	La̱wng Chim	try to taste
มีหนาม	Mi̱-nă̱m	spiny, thorny
มีกลิ่น	Mi̱-glìn	smelly, bad (smell)
มีกลิ่นเหม็น	Mi̱-glìn Měn	bad smell
มีกลิ่นหอม	Mi̱-glìn Hă̱wm	sweet smell

2) Practice saying the following words and phrases:

ดี	Di̱	good
ดีกว่า	Di̱-gwà̱	better
ดีที่สุด	Di̱-tî̱-sùd	best
แพง	Pa̱eng	expensive
แพงกว่า	Pa̱eng-gwà̱	more expensive
แพงที่สุด	Pa̱eng-tî̱-sùd	most expensive
อร่อย	À-rà̱wy	delicious
อร่อยกว่า	À-rà̱wy-gwà̱	more delicious
อร่อยที่สุด	À-rà̱wy-tî̱-sùd	most delicious
มาก	Mâ̱g	many
มากกว่า	Mâ̱g-gwà̱	more
มากที่สุด	Mâ̱g-tî̱-sùd	most
หนาว	Nă̱w	cold
หนาวกว่า	Nă̱w-gwà̱	colder
หนาวที่สุด	Nă̱w-tî̱-sùd	coldest
สวย	Sǔ̱ay	beautiful
สวยกว่า	Sǔ̱ay-gwà̱	more beautiful
สวยที่สุด	Sǔ̱ay-tî̱-sùd	most beautiful

3) Practice saying the following phrases:

ผลไม้ไทย	Pŏn-lâ-mái Tai	Thai fruit
ผลไม้ชนิดไหน	Pŏn-lâ-mái Châ-nîd Năi	what kind of fruit
ผลไม้หลายชนิด	Pŏn-lâ-mái Lăy Châ-nîd	many kinds of fruit
ไม่ชอบผลไม้	Mâi Châwb Pŏn-lâ-mái	do not like fruit
ในฤดูนี้	Nai Rûe-du Nî	in this season
อยากลองชิม	Yàg Lawng Chim	want to try to taste
ชิมทั้งหมด	Chim Táng-mòd	taste them all
ไม่ชอบกลิ่น	Mâi Châwb Glìn	do not like smell
ทนกลิ่นไม่ได้	Ton Glìn Mâi Dâi	can't bear smell
ไม่อยากลอง	Mâi Yàg Lawng	do not want to try

4) Practice saying the following words:

ที่สิบ	Tî-sìb	the tenth
ที่ยี่สิบ	Tî-yî-sìb	the twentieth
ที่ยี่สิบห้า	Tî-yî-sìb-hâ	the twenty-fifth
ที่สามสิบเอ็ด	Tî-săm-sìb-èd	the thirty-first
ที่เจ็ด	Tî-jèd	the seventh
ที่สิบเก้า	Tî-sìb-gâo	the nineteenth
ที่สาม	Tî-săm	the third
ที่สิบสาม	Tî-sìb-săm	the thirteenth
ที่สิบสอง	Tî-sìb-săwng	the twelfth
ที่แปด	Tî-p àed	the eighth
ที่ห้า	Tî-hâ	the fifth

ที่หนึ่ง   Tî-nùeng   the first

5) Practice saying the following sentences:

(1) Kun Sǒn-jai Pǒn-lâ-mái Bâng Mǎi.

(2) Dì-chǎn Mâi Châwb Pǒn-lâ-mái Mâg Nâg.

(3) Kun Mâi Lawng Chim Pǒn-lâ-mái Tai Bâng Rǔe?

(4) Pǒn-lâ-mái Châ-nîd Nǎi?

(5) Mi Pǒn-lâ-mái Lǎy Châ-nîd Nai Rûe-du Ní.

(6) Pǒn-lâ-mái Mi-nǎm Nán Kue À-rai?

(7) Tâ Kun Chim Kun Chaà Châwb.

(8) Man Pen Pǒn-lâ-mai À-ràwy Tî-sùd.

(9) Dì-chǎn Yàg Lawng Chim Kà-nǔn.

(10) Chǔe Plàeg Di.

(11) Lawng Táng-mòd Gâw Dâi.

(12) Kon Tai Châwb Ràb-prà-tan Pǒn-lâ-mǎi.

บทที่ 6 Bòd Tî-Hòg The Sixth Lesson
เดินทางเข้าเมือง Doen-tang Kâo Traveling towards
Mueang the City

1. บทสนทนา / Bòd Sǒn-tâ-na / Conversation

1) ก: ตอนนี้เรากำลังเดินทางเข้าเมือง

T awn-ní Rao Gam-lang Doen-tang Kâo Mueang.

Now we're traveling towards the city.

ข: อยู่ไกลไหมครับ

Yù Glai Mǎi?

Is it far?

2) ก: ไม่ไกลมาก ประมาณยี่สิบห้ากิโลเมตร

Mâi Glai Mâg. Prà-man Yî-sìb-hâ Gì-lo-mêd.

Not very far. About twenty-five kilometers.

ข: อากาศที่นี่ร้อนมาก

A-gàd Tî-nî Ráwn Mâg.

The weather here is very hot.

3) ก: อากาศที่ประเทศของคุณหนาวใช่ไหม

A-gàd Tî Prà-têd Kǎwng-kun Nǎw Châi Mǎi?

The weather in your country is cold, isn't it?

ข: ใช่ หนาวกว่าที่นี่มาก

Châi, Nǎw-gwà Tî-nî Mâg.

Yes, much colder than here.

4) ก: ตอนนี้ที่ประเทศของคุณฤดูอะไร

T awn-ní Tî Prà-têd Kǎwng-kun Rûe-du À-rai?

What season is it now in your country?

ข: ฤดูหนาวซิครับ เพราะอากาศหนาวมาก บางวันมีหิมะตกด้วย

Rûe-du Nǎw Sî Krâb, Prâw A-gàd Nǎw Mâg. Bang Wan Mi Hì-mâ Tòg Dûay.

It's winter, because the weather is very cold. It also snows some days.

5) ก: คุณชอบฤดูหนาวไหมครับ

Kun Châwb Rûe-du Nǎw Mǎi Krâb?

Do you like the winter?

ข: ไม่ชอบเลย ดังนั้นพวกเราจึงมาที่ประเทศของคุณ

Mâi Châwb Loey. Dang-nán Pûag-rao Jueng Ma Tî Prà-têd Kǎwng-kun.

(We) don't like (it) at all. That's why we come to your country.

6) ก: คุณจะพักอยู่ที่นี่นานไหมครับ

Kun Jà Pâg-yù Tî-nî Nan Mǎi?

Will you stay here long?

ช: ประมาณสองสัปดาห์เท่านั้น

Prà-man Sǎwng Sàb-da Tâo-nán.

About two weeks only.

7) ก: พวกเราจะไปภูเก็ตและอยู่ที่นั่นสองสามวัน   แล้วกลับ
ซิดนีย์

Pûag-rao Jà Pai Pu-gèd Lâe Yù Tî-nân Sǎwng-sǎm Wan,
Láew Glàb Sîd-nî.

We will go to Phuket and stay there a few days, then go
back to Sydney.

2. คำศัพท์ / Kam-sab / Vocabulary

เดินทาง	Doen-tang	travel, traveling
เข้า	Kâo	towards
เมือง	Mueang	city
อยู่	Yù	stay
ไกล	Glai	far
ไม่ไกล	Mâi Glai	not far
ประมาณ	Prà-man	about, approxi-mately
ยี่สิบห้า	Yî-sìb-hâ	twenty-five
กิโลเมตร	Gì-lo-mêd	kilometer
อากาศ	A-gàd	weather
ที่นี่	Tî-nî	here
ร้อน	Ráwn	hot
หนาว	Nǎw	cold

ประเทศ	Prà-têd	country
ของคุณ	Kǎwng-kun	your
หนาวกว่า	Nǎw-gwà	colder
ฤดู	Rûe-du	season
ฤดูหนาว	Rûe-du Nǎw	winter, cold season
ซิ	Sî	of course
เพราะ	Prâw	because
บาง	Bang	some
วัน	Wan	day
บางวัน	Bang Wan	some days
หิมะ	Hì-mâ	snow
ตก	Tòg	fall
ด้วย	Dûay	also, too, as well
ชอบ	Châwb	like
ไม่ชอบ	Mâi Châwb	do not like
ไม่ชอบเลย	Mâi Châwb Loey	do not like at all
ดังนั้นจึง	Dang-nán...Jueng	That's why, there-fore
มา	Ma	come
มาที่	Ma Tî	come to
พักอยู่	Pâg-yù	stay
นาน	Nan	long (time)
สอง	Sǎwng	two
สัปดาห์	Sàb-da	week
เท่านั้น	Tâo-nán	only
ที่นี่	Tî-nî	here
ที่นั่น	Tî-nân	there

ภูเก็ต	Pu-gèd	Phuket
สองสาม	Săwng-săm	few
แล้ว	Láew	then
กลับ	Glàb	go back, return
ซิดนีย์	Sîd-nî	Sydney
ร้อย	Ráwy	hundred
พัน	Pan	thousand
หมื่น	Mùen	ten thousand
แสน	Săen	hundred thousand
ล้าน	Lán	million

3. หลักไวยากรณ์ / Làg Wai-ya-gawn / Grammar Points

1) กำลัง Gam-lang: a particle to add in front of a verb to indicate the action is on-going. It is similar to English 'be' plus verb with '-ing'.

ไป	Pai	go
กำลังไป	Gam-lang Pai	(be) going
มา	Ma	come
กำลังมา	Gam-lang Ma	(be) coming
กิน	Gin	eat
กำลังกิน	Gam-lang Gin	(be) eating

(1) ตอนนี้เรากำลังเดินทางเข้าเมือง

Tawn-ní Rao Gam-lang Doen-tang Kâo Mueang.

Now we are traveling towards the city.

(2) เขากำลังมา

Kăo Gam-lang Ma.

He is coming.

(3) พวกเขากำลังไปที่นั่น

Pûag-kǎo Gam-lang Pai Tî-nân.

They are going there.

2) ของ Kǎwng: a particle added in front of personal pronouns to become possessive pronouns.

ของผม	Kǎwng-pǒm	my (used by males)
ของฉัน	Kǎwng-chǎn	my (used by females)
ของดิฉัน	Kǎwng-dì-chǎn	
ของคุณ	Kǎwng-kun	your
ของเขา (ผู้ชาย)	Kǎwng-kǎo	his
ของเขา (ผู้หญิง)	Kǎwng-kǎo	her
ของมัน	Kǎwng-man	its
ของพวกเรา,	Kǎwng-pûag-rao,	our
ของเรา	Kǎwng-rao	
ของพวกคุณ,	Kǎwng-pûag-kun,	your
ของคุณ	Kǎwng-kun	
ของพวกเขา,	Kǎwng-pûag-kǎo,	their
ของเขา	Kǎwng-kǎo	

3) การนับ Gan-nab = counting. The cardinal numbers in Thai are as follows:

1	หนึ่ง	Nùeng
2	สอง	Sǎwng
3	สาม	Sǎm
4	สี่	Sì
5	ห้า	Hâ
6	หก	Hòg

7	เจ็ด	Jèd
8	แปด	P̲ àed
9	เก้า	Gâo
10	สิบ	Sìb
11	สิบเอ็ด	Sìb-èd
12	สิบสอง	Sìb-s̲ǎw̲ng
13	สิบสาม	Sìb-s̲ǎm
14	สิบสี่	Sìb-s̲ì
15	สิบห้า	Sìb-h̲â
16	สิบหก	Sìb-hòg
17	สิบเจ็ด	Sìb-jèd
18	สิบแปด	Sìb-p̲ àed
19	สิบเก้า	Sìb-gâo
20	ยี่สิบ	Yî̲-sìb
21	ยี่สิบเอ็ด	Yî̲-sìb-èd
22	ยี่สิบสอง	Yî̲-sìb-s̲ǎw̲ng
23	ยี่สิบสาม	Yî̲-sìb-s̲ǎm
24	ยี่สิบสี่	Yî̲-sìb-s̲ì
25	ยี่สิบห้า	Yî̲-sìb-h̲â
26	ยี่สิบหก	Yî̲-sìb-hòg
27	ยี่สิบเจ็ด	Yî̲-sìb-jèd
28	ยี่สิบแปด	Yî̲-sìb-p̲ àed
29	ยี่สิบเก้า	Yî̲-sìb-gâo
30	สามสิบ	S̲ǎm-sìb
31	สามสิบเอ็ด	S̲ǎm-sìb-èd
40	สี่สิบ	S̲ì-sìb
41	สี่สิบเอ็ด	S̲ì-sìb-èd

50	ห้าสิบ	Hâ-sìb
51	ห้าสิบเอ็ด	Hâ-sìb-èd
90	เก้าสิบ	Gâo-sìb
91	เก้าสิบเอ็ด	Gâo-sìb-èd
100	(หนึ่ง) ร้อย	(Nùeng)-ráwy
200	สองร้อย	Sǎwng-ráwy
300	สามร้อย	Sǎm-ráwy
1,000	(หนึ่ง)พัน	(Nùeng)-pan
2,000	สองพัน	Sǎwng-pan
5,000	ห้าพัน	Hâ-pan
10,000	(หนึ่ง)หมื่น	(Nùeng)-mùen
20,000	สองหมื่น	Sǎwng-mùen
60,000	หกหมื่น	Hòg-mùen
100,000	(หนึ่ง)แสน	(Nùeng)-sǎen
300,000	สามแสน	Sǎm-sǎen
700,000	เจ็ดแสน	Jèd-sǎen
1,000,000	(หนึ่ง)ล้าน	(Nùeng)-lán
5,000,000	ห้าล้าน	Hâ-lán
9,000,000	เก้าล้าน	Gâo-lán
10,000,000	สิบล้าน	Sìb-lán
50,000,000	ห้าสิบล้าน	Hâ-sìb-lán
100,000,000	ร้อยล้าน	Ráwy-lán

4. แบบฝึกหัด / Bàeb-fùeg-hàd / Exercises

1) Practice saying the following words:

เดินทาง	Doen-tang	travel
ตอนนี้	Tawn-ní	now

กำลัง	Gam-lang	(be) plus verb with 'ing'
ไม่ไกล	Mâi Glai	not far
ประมาณ	Prà-m<u>a</u>n	about, approximately
กิโลเมตร	Gì-l<u>o</u>-mê̱d	kilometer
อากาศ	<u>A</u>-gàd	weather
หนาวกว่า	N<u>ǎ</u>w-gw<u>à</u>	colder
ของคุณ	K<u>ǎw</u>ng-kun	your
ของผม	K<u>ǎw</u>ng-p<u>ǒ</u>m	my
สัปดาห์	Sàb-d<u>a</u>	week
พักอยู่	Pâg-y<u>ù</u>	stay
หลังจาก	Lang-j<u>à</u>g	after
ภูเก็ต	P<u>u</u>-gèd	Phuket
ซิดนีย์	Sî̱d-n<u>î</u>	Sydney

2) Practice saying the following words:

หนาว	N<u>ǎ</u>w	cold
หนาวกว่า	N<u>ǎ</u>w-gw<u>à</u>	colder
ร้อน	Rá<u>w</u>n	hot
ร้อนกว่า	Rá<u>w</u>n-gwà	hotter
ไกล	Glai	far
ไกลกว่า	Glai-gw<u>à</u>	farther, further
ใกล้	Glâi	near
ใกล้กว่า	Glâi-gw<u>à</u>	nearer

3) Practice counting the following numbers in Thai:

25	ยี่สิบห้า	Yî̱-sìb-h<u>â</u>
30	สามสิบ	S<u>ǎ</u>m-s<u>ì</u>b

78	เจ็ดสิบแปด	Jèd-sìb-p àed
91	เก้าสิบเอ็ด	Gâo-sìb-èd
105	หนึ่งร้อยห้า	Nùeng-ráwy-hâ
350	สามร้อยห้าสิบ	Săm-ráwy-hâ-sìb
7,250	เจ็ดพันสองร้อยห้าสิบ	Jèd-pan-săwng-ráwy-hâ-sìb
6,732	หกพันเจ็ดร้อยสามสิบสอง	Hòg-pan-jèd-ráwy-săm-sìb-săwng
10,000	หนึ่งหมื่น	Nùeng-mùen
20,500	สองหมื่นห้าร้อย	Săwng-mùen-hâ-ráwy
96,340	เก้าหมื่นหกพันสามร้อยสี่สิบ	Gâo-mùen-hòg-pan-săm-ráwy-sì-sìb
100,000	หนึ่งแสน	Nùeng-săen
253,000	สองแสนห้าหมื่นสามพัน	Săwng-săen-hâ-mùen-săm-pan
876,550	แปดแสนเจ็ดหมื่นหกพันห้าร้อยห้าสิบ	P àed-săen-jèd-mùen-hòg-pan-hâ-ráwy-hâ-sìb
1,000,000	หนึ่งล้าน	Nùeng-lán
5,500,000	ห้าล้านห้าแสน	Hâ-lán-hâ-săen
12,000,000	สิบสองล้าน	Sìb-săwng-lán

4) Practice saying the following phrases:

บ้านของผม	Bân Kăwng-pŏm	my house
เสื้อของคุณ	Sûea Kăwng-kun	your shirt
รถของเขา	Rôd Kăwng-kăo	his car

ภรรยาของคุณ	Pan-y<u>a</u> K<u>ǎ</u>wng-kun	your wife
สามีของดิฉัน	Sǎ-m<u>i</u> K<u>ǎ</u>wng-dì-chǎn	my husband
ประเทศของคุณ	<u>P</u>rà-t<u>ê</u>d K<u>ǎ</u>wng-kun	your country
เพื่อนของเรา	P<u>û</u>ean Kǎwng-rao	our friends
ร้านอาหาร	R<u>á</u>n-<u>a</u>-h<u>ǎ</u>n	our restaurant
ของพวกเขา	Kǎwng-p<u>û</u>ag-rao	

5) Practice saying the following dialogue:

(1) A: <u>A</u>-g<u>à</u>d R<u>á</u>wn Châi Mǎi?

   B: Châi, <u>A</u>-g<u>à</u>d R<u>á</u>wn M<u>â</u>g.

(2) A: <u>A</u>-g<u>à</u>d Tî-n<u>î</u> N<u>ǎ</u>w Châi Mǎi?

   B: Mâi, <u>A</u>-g<u>à</u>d Tî-n<u>î</u> Mâi Nǎw L<u>o</u>ey.

(3) A: Kun M<u>a</u> Jàg <u>P</u>rà-t<u>ê</u>d K<u>a</u>-n<u>a</u>-d<u>a</u> Châi Mǎi?

   B: Mâi Châi, Pǒm M<u>a</u> Jàg A-me-r<u>î</u>-ga.

(4) A: Kun Mâi Ch<u>â</u>wb Rûe-d<u>u</u> N<u>ǎ</u>w Châi Mǎi?

   B: Pǒm Mâi Ch<u>â</u>wb <u>A</u>-g<u>à</u>d Nǎw M<u>â</u>g Nâg.

(5) A: Kun P<u>â</u>g-y<u>ù</u> Tî-n<u>î</u> Châi Mǎi?

   B: Krâb, Pǒm P<u>â</u>g-y<u>ù</u> Tî-n<u>î</u>.

6) Practice saying the following sentences:

(1) T <u>a</u>wn-n<u>í</u> Rao Gam-lang D<u>oe</u>n-t<u>a</u>ng Kâo M<u>uea</u>ng.

(2) Y<u>ù</u> Glai Mǎi?

(3) Mâi Glai M<u>â</u>g. <u>P</u>rà-m<u>a</u>n Yî-sìb-h<u>â</u> Gì-l<u>o</u>-m<u>ê</u>d

(4) <u>A</u>-g<u>à</u>d Tî-n<u>î</u> R<u>á</u>wn M<u>â</u>g.

(5) <u>A</u>-g<u>à</u>d Tî <u>P</u>rà-t<u>ê</u>d Kǎwng-pǒm Nǎw-gwà Tî-n<u>î</u> M<u>â</u>g.

(6) B<u>a</u>ng Wan M<u>i</u> Hì-m<u>â</u> <u>T</u>òg Nai Rûe-d<u>u</u> Nǎw.

(7) Kun Jà P<u>â</u>g-y<u>ù</u> Tî-n<u>î</u> N<u>a</u>n Mǎi?

บทที่ 7   Bòd Tî-jèd   The Seventh Lesson
เที่ยวชมสถานที่   Tîaw-chom   Sightseeing
สำคัญ   Sà-tăn-tî
    Săm-kan

1. บทสนทนา / Bòd Sŏn-tâ-na / Conversation

1) ก: คุณพร้อมจะไปเที่ยวชมสถานที่สำคัญหรือยัง   วันนี้
เป็นวันอาทิตย์ สถานที่หลายแห่งเปิดให้คนเข้าชม

Kun Práwm Jà Pai Tîaw-chom Sà-tăn-tî Săm-kan Rŭe
Yang? Wan-ní Pen Wan-a-tîd. Sà-tăn-tî Lăy Hàeng P òed
Hâi Kon Kâo-chom.

Are you ready to go sightseeing? Today is Sunday.
Many places are open for people to visit.

ข: ครับพวกเราพร้อมแล้ว แต่รอประเดี๋ยว ภรรยาของ
ผมลืมกล้องถ่ายรูปไว้ในห้อง

Krâb, Pûag-rao Práwm Láew. Tàe Raw Prà-dǐaw. Pan-
ya Kǎwng-pǒm Luem Glâwng-tày-rûb Wái Nai Hâwng.

Yes, we're ready. But wait a minute. My wife left the
camera in the room.

2) ก: เราจะไปที่ไหนก่อน มีที่น่าสนใจหลายแห่งเหลือเกิน

Rao Ja Pai Tî-nǎi Gàwn? Mi Tî Nâ-sǒn-jai Lǎy Hàeng
Lǔea-goen.

Where will we go first? There are so many interesting
places.

ข: เราจะไปวัดเบญจมบพิตรก่อน เพราะอยู่ไม่ไกลจากที่นี่
ผมดูจากแผนที่

Rao Ja Pai Wâd Ben-ja-mâ-baw-pîd Gàwn, Prâw Yù Mâi
Glai Jàg Tî-nî. Pǒm Du Jàg Pǎen-tî.

We'll go to the Marble Temple first, for it's not far from
here. I (will) look at the map.

3) ก: ดีแล้วพวกเราจะไปที่นั่นหลังจากนั้นคุณอยากไปไหนต่อ

Di Láew Pûag-rao Jà Pai Tî-nân. Lǎng-jàg Nán Kun Yàg
Pai Nǎi T àw?

Good enough, we will go there. After that, where do you
want to go next?

ข: ขอดูแผนที่อีกครั้ง พวกเราไปพระบรมมหาราชวัง วัด
พระแก้ว และวัดโพธิ์ดีไหม ทั้งหมดนี้อยู่บริเวณเดียวกัน

Kǎw Du Pǎen-tî îg-kráng. Pûag-rao Pai Prâ Baw-rom-mâ-
hǎ Râd-châ-wang, Wâd Prâ Gâew, Lâe Wâd Po Di Mǎi?
Táng-mòd Ní Yù Baw-rî-wen Diaw-gan.

Let me see the map once again. We (shall) go to the Grand Palace, Wat Phra Kaeo, and Wat Pho, shall we? All of these are in the same compound.

ก: เราไปได้ทั้งวันถ้ายังดูไม่หมด   ผมพาคุณไปได้ทั้งวันเหมือนกัน

Rao Pai Dâi Táng Wan Tâ Yang Du Mâi Mòd. Pǒm Pa Kun Pai Dâi Táng Wan Mǔean-gan.

We can go all day if we still can't see all (of these places in a short time). I can take you all day as well.

ข: ดีทีเดียว พวกเรามีเวลาน้อย วันจันทร์หน้าจะเดินทางต่อแล้ว

Di Ti-diaw. Pûag-rao Mi We-la Náwy. Wan-jan Nâ Jà Doen-tang T àw Láew.

Quite good. We have little time. Next Monday we will have to continue traveling.

5) ก: เราควรไปเดี๋ยวนี้เลย เราจะได้มีเวลานาน ๆ ในแต่ละแห่ง

Rao Kuan Pai Dǐaw-ní Loey. Rao Jà Dâi Mi We-la Nan-nan Nai Tàe-lâ Hàeng.

We should go right away. We will have a long time in each place.

ข: ใช่แล้ว เราควรไปแต่เช้า ภรรยาของผมลงมาแล้ว

Châi Láew, Rao Kuan Pai T àe-cháo. Pan-ya Kǎwng-pǒm Long-ma Láew.

Right, we should go early. My wife has come down.

6) ก: เชิญไปที่รถได้เลย   รถของผมจอดอยู่ที่ลานจอดรถด้านหลังโรงแรม

Choen Pai Tî Rôd Dâi Loey. Rôd Kăwng-pŏm Jàwd Yù-
tî Lan-jàwd-rôd Dân-lăng Rong-raem.

Please go ahead to my car. My car is parked in the parking lot behind the hotel.

ข: มีอะไรอยู่ที่วัดเบญจมบพิตร น่าสนใจมากไหม

Mi À-rai Yù Tî Wâd Ben-jà-mâ-baw-pîd? Na-sŏn-jai Mâg Măi?

What is there (to see) at the Marble Temple? (Is it) very interesting?

7) ก: มีหลายอย่าง น่าสนใจทั้งนั้น เมื่อคุณไปถึงคุณจะเห็น เอง คุณจะแวะที่ไหนก่อนไหม

Mi Lăy Yàng. Nâ-sŏn-jai Táng-nán. Mûea Kun Pai-tŭeng Kun Jà Hĕn Eng. Kun Jà Wâe Tî-năi Gàwn Măi?

There are many things. All (of them) are interesting. When you arrive, you will see for yourself. Would you like to drop in anywhere first?

ข: พวกเราต้องการแวะที่ร้านถ่ายรูปซื้อฟิล์ม เราอาจจะ ใช้ฟิล์มหลายม้วน

Pûag-rao Tâwng-gan Wâe Tî Rán-tày-rûb Súe Fim. Rao Àd-ja Chái Fim Lăy Múan.

We'd like to drop in at the photo shop to buy some film. We may use many rolls of film.

2. คำศัพท์ / Kam-sàb / Vocabulary

เที่ยว	Tîaw	tour, visit
ชมสถานที่	Chom Sà-tăn-tî-	sightseeing
สำคัญ	Săm-kan	

ชม	Chom	admire
พร้อม	Práwm	ready
พร้อมจะไป	Práwm Jà Pai	ready to go
สถานที่	Sà-tăn-tîî	place
สำคัญ	Săm-kan	important
ยัง	Yang	still, yet
วันอาทิตย์	Wan-a-tîîd	Sunday
เปิด	P òed	open
เข้าชม	Kâo-chom	visit
รอ	Raw	wait
ประเดี๋ยว	Pra-dĭaw	a minute
ภรรยา	Pan-ya	wife
ของผม	Kăwng-pŏm	my
ลืม...ไว้	Luem...Wái	leave, left
กล้องถ่ายรูป	Glâwng-tày-rûb	camera
ใน	Nai	in
ห้อง	Hâwng	room
ที่ไหน, ไหน	Tîî-năi, Năi	where
ก่อน	Gàwn	first
ที่ สถานที่	Tîî, Sà-tăn-tîî	place
น่าสนใจ	Nâ-sŏn-jai	interesting
หลาย	Lăy	many
เหลือเกิน	Lŭea-goen	so many
วัด	Wâd	monastery, Buddhist temple
เบญจมบพิตร	Ben-jà-mâ-baw-pîd	the Marble Temple
อยู่	Yùu	is

ไม่ไกล	Mâi Glai	not far
จาก	Jàg	from
ที่นี่	Tî-nî	here
ดู	Du	look
แผนที่	Păen-tî	map
ดีแล้ว	Di-láew	good enough
อยาก	Yàg	want
ไป...ต่อ	Pai...Tàw	go next
อีกครั้ง	Ìg-kráng	once again
พระบรม มหาราชวัง	Prâ-Baw-rom-mâ-hă Râd-châ-wang	the Grand Palace
วัดพระแก้ว	Wâd Prâ Gâew	the Emerald Buddha Temple Wat Phra Kaeo
วัดโพธิ์	Wâd Po	the Reclining Buddha Temple Wat Pho
ดีไหม	Di-măi	shall we?
ไป...ดีไหม	Pai...Di-măi	Shall we go?
ทั้งหมด	Táng-mòd	all
ทั้งหมดนี้	Táng-mòd Nî	all of these
บริเวณ	Baw-rî-wen	compound, enclosure
เดียวกัน	Diaw-gan	the same
ทั้งวัน	Táng Wan	all day
ยัง	Yang	still
ไม่หมด	Mâi Mòd	not all

พา...ไป	Pa...Pai	take... to go
เหมือนกัน	Mǔean-gan	also, as well
ดีทีเดียว	Di Ti-diaw	quite good
เวลา	We-la	time
น้อย	Náwy	little
วันจันทร์	Wan-jan	Monday
หน้า	Nâ	next
วันจันทร์หน้า	Wan-jan Nâ	next Monday
เดินทาง	Doen-tang	travel
เดินทางต่อ	Doen-tang Tàw	continue traveling
ควร	Kuan	should
ควรไป	Kuan Pai	should go
นานๆ	Nan-nan	long (time)
แต่ละ	Tàe-lâ	each
แต่ละแห่ง	Tàe-lâ Hàeng	each place
ใช่แล้ว	Châi Láew	that's right
แต่เช้า	Tàe-cháo	early
ลงมา	Long-ma	come down
ลงมาแล้ว	Long-ma Láew	has come down
เชิญ	Choen	please
เชิญไป	Choen Pai	please go
จอด	Jàwd	park (a car)
ลานจอดรถ	Lan-jàwd-rôd	parking lot
ด้านหลัง	Dân-lǎng	behind
โรงแรม	Rong-raem	hotel
มี	Mi	there is/ there are
อะไร	À-rai	what

ทั้งนั้น	Táng-nán	all
เมื่อ	Mûea	when
ไปถึง	Pai-tŭeng	arrive
เห็น	Hĕn	see
เอง	Eng	self
แวะ	Wâe	drop in
ก่อน	Gàwn	first
ร้าน	Rán	shop, store
ถ่ายรูป	Tày-rûb	taking pictures
ร้านถ่ายรูป	Rán-tày-rûb	photo shop
รูปถ่าย	Rûb-tày	picture, photo-graph, photo
ซื้อ	Súe	buy
ฟิล์ม	Fim	film
ม้วน	Múan	roll
ฟิล์มหลายม้วน	Fim Lăy Múan	many rolls of film
อาจจะ, อาจ	Àd-jà, Àd	may
ใช้	Chái	use

3. หลักไวยากรณ์ / Làg Wai-ya-gawn / Grammar Points

1) เอง Eng = self, a reflexive pronoun, placed after any personal pronoun, or at the end of the sentence.

ผมเอง	Pŏm-eng	myself (used by males)
ดิฉันเอง	Dì-chăn-eng	myself (used by females)
คุณเอง	Kun-eng	yourself

เขาเอง	Kǎo-eng	himself, herself
มันเอง	Man-eng	itself
พวกเราเอง	Pûag-rao-eng	ourselves
พวกคุณเอง	Pûag-kun-eng	yourselves
พวกเขาเอง	Pûag-kǎo-eng	themselves
ผม...เอง	Pǒm...Eng	... myself, etc.

(1) พวกเราเองต้องการไปที่นั่น

Pûag-rao-eng T âwng-gan Pai Tî-nân.

We ourselves want to go there.

(2) เขาเองอยากพบคุณ

Kǎo-eng Yàg Pôb Kun.

He himself wants to meet you.

(3) ผมทำเอง

Pǒm Tam Eng

I do it myself.

(4) คุณจะเห็นเอง

Kun Jà Hěn Eng.

You will see it yourself.

2) วัน Wan = day; the days of the week and other days are expressed as follows:

วันอาทิตย์	Wan-a-tîd	Sunday
วันจันทร์	Wan-jan	Monday
วันอังคาร	Wan-ang-kan	Tuesday
วันพุธ	Wan-pûd	Wednesday
วันพฤหัสบดี	Wan-pâ-rûe-hàd-baw-di	Thursday
วันศุกร์	Wan-sùg	Friday

วันเสาร์	Wan-sǎo	Saturday
วันหยุด	Wan-yùd	holiday, vacation
วันพระ	Wan-prâ	Buddhist Holy Day
วันเกิด	Wan-gòed	birthday
วันชาติ	Wan-châd	national day
วันแรงงาน	Wan-raeng-ngan	Labor Day

4. แบบฝึกหัด / Bàeb-fùeg-hàd / Exercises

1) Practice saying the following words:

พร้อม	Práwm	ready
พร้อมจะไป	Práwm Jà Pai	ready to go
สำคัญ	Sǎm-kan	important
สถานที่	Sà-tǎn-tî	place
สถานที่สำคัญ	Sà-tǎn-tî Sǎm-kan	important place
เข้าชม	Kâo-chom	visit
แผนที่	Pǎen-tî	map
กล้อง	Glâwng	camera
กล้องถ่ายรูป	Glâwng-tày-rûb	camera
รูปถ่าย	Rûb-tày	picture, photograph
ถ่ายรูป	Tày-rûb	take picture
ร้านถ่ายรูป	Rán-tày-rûb	photo shop
ฟิล์ม	Fim	film
ฟิล์มหลาย ม้วน	Fim Lǎy Múan	many rolls of film

2) Practice saying the following words and phrases:

ดีแล้ว	Di Láew	good enough
ดีทีเดียว	Di Ti-diaw	quite good

ทั้งหมด	Táng-mòd	all
ทั้งหมดนี้	Táng-mòd Ní	all of these
ทั้งวัน	Táng-wan	all day
ทั้งวันทั้งคืน	Táng-wan Tâng-kuen	all day, all night
ด้านหลัง	Dân-lăng	behind
ลานจอดรถ	Lan-jàwd-rôd	parking lot
แต่ละแห่ง	T áe-lâ Hàeng	each place
บริเวณ	Baw-rî-wen	compound, enclosure
บริเวณเดียวกัน	Baw-rî-wen Diaw-gan	the same compound
วันจันทร์หน้า	Wan-jan Nâ	next Monday
เดินทางต่อ	Doen-tang T àw	continue traveling

3) Try to remember the days of the week as follows:

วันอาทิตย์	Wan-a-tîd	Sunday
วันจันทร์	Wan-jan	Monday
วันอังคาร	Wan-ang-kan	Tuesday
วันพุธ	Wan-pûd	Wednesday
วันพฤหัสบดี	Wan-pâ-rûe-hàd-baw-di	Thursday
วันศุกร์	Wan Sùg	Friday
วันเสาร์	Wan Săo	Saturday

4) Practice saying the following dialogue:

(1) ก: คุณจะเห็นเอง

Kun Jà Hĕn Eng.

You will see it yourself.

ข: ผมเองจะเห็นได้อย่างไร

Pŏm-eng Ja Hĕn Dâi Yàng-rai?

How can I see it myself?

(2) ก: คุณเองพูดไทยได้ดี

Kun-eng Pûd Tai Dâi Di.

You yourself speak Thai well.

ข: ผมเองยังพูดเช่นนั้นไม่ได้

Pŏm-eng Yang Pûd Chên Nán Mâi Dâi.

I myself cannot say that.

(3) ก: เขาพูดว่าเขาจะมาเอง

Kăo Pûd Wâ Kăo Jà Ma Eng.

He said that he would come (by) himself.

ข: คุณเองไม่ฟังผม

Kun-eng Mâi Fang Pŏm.

You yourself don't listen to me.

(4) ก: ใครว่าเขาจะไปเอง

Krai Wâ Kăo Jà Pai Eng?

Who said he would go (by) himself?

ข: เขาเองบอกผมเมื่อวานนี้

Kăo-eng Bàwg Pŏm Mûea-wan Ní.

He himself told me yesterday.

(5) ก: ใครจะไปที่นั่น

Krai Jà Pai Tî-nân?

Who will go there?

ข: พวกเราเองจะไปที่นั่น

Pûag-rao-eng Jà Pai Tî-nân.

We ourselves will go there.

(6) ก: ใครเชิญเขามาที่นี่

Krai Choen Kǎo Ma Tî-nî?

Who invites him to come here?

ช: เขามาเอง

Kǎo Ma Eng.

He comes (by) himself.

5) Practice saying the following sentences:

(1) Kun Práwm Jà Pai Tîaw-chom Sà-tǎn-tî Sǎm-kan Rǔe Yang?

(2) Wan-nî Pen Wan-a-tìd.

(3) Sa-tǎn-tî Lǎy Hàeng Pòed Hâi Kon Kâo-chom.

(4) Krâb, Pûag-rao Práwm Láew.

(5) T àe Raw Prà-dǐaw.

(6) Pan-ya Kǎwng-pǒm Luem Glâwng-tày-rûb Wái Nai Hâwng.

(7) Rao Jà Pai Tî-nǎi Gàwn?

(8) Mi Tî Nâ-sǒn-jai Lǎy Hàeng Lǔea-goen.

(9) Rao Jà Pai Wâd Ben-jà-mâ-baw-pîd Gàwn.

(10) Prâw Yù Mâi Glai Jàg Tî-nî.

(11) Pǒm Du Jàg Pàen-tî.

(12) Di Láew Pûag-rao Jà Pai Tî-nân.

(13) Lǎng-jàg Nán Kun Yàg Pai Nǎi T àw?

(14) Kǎw Du Pǎen-tî Ìg-kráng.

(15) Pûag-rao Pai Prâ Baw-rom-mâ-hǎ Râd-châ-wang.

(16) Pûag-rao Pai Wâd Prâ Gâew Lâe Wâd Po Di Mǎi?

(17) Táng-mòd Ní Yù Baw-rî-wen Diaw-gan.

(18) Rao Pâi Dai Táng-wan Tâ Yang Du Mâi Mòd.

(19) Pǒm Pa Kun Pai Dâi Táng-wan Mǔean-gan.

(20) Dị Ti-dịạw.

(21) Pûạg-rao Mị Wẹ-lạ Nảwy.

(22) Wan-jan Nâ Jà Dọen-tạng T àw Láew.

(23) Rao Kụan Pại Dĭaw-nị́ Lọey.

(24) Rao Jà Dâi Mị Wẹ-lạ Nan-nạn Nai T àe-lâ Hàẹng.

(25) Châi Láew, Rao Kụan Pại T àe-cháo.

(26) Pan-yạ Kăẉ̆ng-pŏm Long-mạ Láew.

(27) Chọen Pại Tî Rôd Dâi Lọey.

(28) Rôd Kăwng-pŏm Jàẉd Yù-tî̂ Lan-jàẉd-rôd.

(29) Kun Jà Wâe Tî̂-năi Gàẉn Măi?

(30) Wâe Rán-tày-rûb Súe Fịm Lăy Múạn.

บทที่ 8   Bòd Tî-Pàed   The Eighth Lesson
ที่วัดเบญจ   Tî Wad Ben-jà-   At the Marble
มบพิตร   mâ-baw-pîd   Temple

1. บทสนทนา / Bòd Sŏn-tâ-na / Conversation

1) ก: นี่คือวัดเบญจมบพิตร โบสถ์ทำด้วยหินอ่อนจาก
ประเทศอิตาลี

Nî Kue Wâd Ben-jà-mâ-baw-pîd. Bòd Tam-dûay Hĭn-àwn
Jàg Prà-têd Ì-t a-li

This is the Marble Temple. The temple is made of marble
from Italy.

ข: สวยมากจริงๆ อะไรอยู่ในนั้น

Sŭay Mâg Jing-jing. À-rai Yù Nai Nán?

Very beautiful indeed. What's in that (temple)?

2) ก: มีพระพุทธรูปน่าสนใจและมีพระสงฆ์อยู่เป็นจำนวนมาก
โดยเฉพาะระหว่างเข้าพรรษา

Mi Prâ Pûd-tâ-rûb Nâ-sŏn-jai Lâe Mi Prâ-sŏng Yù Pen-
jam-nuan Mâg, Doy-chà-pâw Ra-wàng Kâo-pan-sǎ.

There are interesting Buddha images, and there is a
great number of Buddhist monks, especially during the
Buddhist Lent.

ข: คุณว่าอะไรนะ 'เข้าพรรษา' หมายถึงอะไร

Kun Wâ A-rai Nâ? "Kâo Pan-sǎ" Mǎy-tǔeng À-rai?

What's this you say? What does "the Buddhist Lent"
mean?

3) ก: เป็นช่วงที่พระสงฆ์ต้องอยู่ประจำที่วัด ท่านไปค้างแรม
ที่อื่นไม่ได้ ประมาณสามเดือน ตั้งแต่กรกฎาคมถึง
กันยายน

Pen Chûang Tî Prâ-sŏng T âwng Yù Prà-jam Tî Wâd. Tân
Pai Káng-raem Tî Ùen Mâi Dâi Prà-man Sǎm Duean,
Tâng-t àe Gaw-râ-gà-da-kom Tǔeng Gan-ya-yon.

It's the period in which the monks have to stay permanently at the monastery. They cannot go to stay overnight anywhere else for about three months, from July to
September.

ข: พระสงฆ์ทำอะไรในระหว่างเข้าพรรษา

Prâ-sŏng Tam À-rai Nai Râ-wàng Kâo Pan-sǎ?

What do the monks do during the Buddhist Lent?

4) ก: ท่านจะศึกษาธรรมะ คำสั่งสอนของพระพุทธเจ้า
ปฏิบัติตามคำสั่งสอนนั้น นอกจากนี้ท่านจะช่วยดูแล
บริเวณวัด

Tân Jà Sùeg-sǎ Tam-mâ, Kam-sàng-sǎwn Kǎwng Prâ Pûd-tâ-jâo, Pà-tì-bàd T am Kam-sàng-sǎwn Nán. Nâwg-jàg-ní Tân Jà Chûay Du-lae Baw-rî-wen Wâd.

They will study Dhamma, the Lord Buddha's Teachings, (and) practice (them) accordingly; in addition, they'll help take care of the temple.

ข: พระพุทธศาสนาน่าสนใจมาก พวกเราอยากรู้เรื่องมาก กว่านี้ เราเข้าไปข้างในโบสถ์ได้ไหม

Prâ Pûd-tâ-sǎd-sà-nǎ Nâ-sǒn-jai Mâg. Pûag-rao Yàg Rú-rûeang Mâg-gwà Ní. Rao Kâo Pai Kâng-nai Bòd Dâi Mai?

Buddhism is very interesting. We'd like to know more about it. Can we go inside the temple?

5) ก: ได้ซิครับ   แต่กรุณารอประเดี๋ยว   ผมไปซื้อบัตรผ่าน ประตูก่อน

Dâi Sî Krâb. T àe Ga-rû-na Raw Prà-dǐaw. Pǒm Pai Súe Bad-pàn-prà-t u Gàwn.

Of course, you can. But please wait just a minute. I (will) go to buy the admission tickets first.

ข: ให้พวกเราซื้อได้ไหม คุณพาพวกเรามาที่นี่

Hâi Pûag-rao Súe Dâi Mǎi: Kun Pa Pûag-rao Ma Tî-nî.

Can we buy them? You brought us here.

6) ก: ไม่เป็นไรครับ นิดหน่อยเท่านั้น เชิญมาทางนี้ คุณจะ ถ่ายรูปตรงนี้ก่อนก็ได้

Mâi Pen-rai. Nîd-nàwy Tâo-nán. Choen Ma Tang Ní. Kun Jà Tày-rûb Trong-nî Gàwn Gâw Dâi.

Never mind. It (costs) just a little. Please come this way. You can just as well take pictures right here.

ข: ให้ผมถ่ายรูปคุณด้วย   มุมนี้สวยมากถ้ามีคุณอยู่ด้วย
คุณแต่งตัวดี รูปจะออกมากน่ารัก

Hâi Pǒm Tày-rûb Kun Dûay. Mum Ní Sǔay Mâg Tâ Mi Kun
Yù Dûay. Kun T àeng-t ua Di. Rûb Jà Àwg-ma Nâ-râg.

Let me take your pictures too. (A shot from) this angle is
very beautiful if you're in it too. You're well dressed (and
thus) the picture will turn out to be pretty.

7) ก: ขอบคุณสำหรับคำชม เชิญถ่ายรูปโบสถ์อย่างเดียวก็พอ
ที่นี่เชิญเข้าไปข้างใน

Kàwb-kun Sǎm-ràb Kam-chom. Choen Tày-rûb Bòd
Yàng-diaw Gâw Paw. Ti-ní Choen Kâo-pai Kâng-nai.

Thank you for your compliments. It's enough just to take
pictures of the temple. Now, please go inside.

ข: โอ้โฮ มีพระพุทธรูปมากจริง ๆ น่าสนใจมาก ผมกลัว
ว่าฟิล์มจะไม่พอถ่ายรูปที่นี่

Ô-ho! Mi Prâ Pûd-tâ-rûb Mâg Jing-jing! Nâ-sǒn-jai Mâg.
Pǒm Glua Wâ Fim Jà Mâi Paw Tày-rûb Tî-nî.

Wow! There are such a lot of Buddha images! It's very
interesting. I'm afraid that there will not be enough film to
take pictures here.

2. คำศัพท์ / Kam-sàb / Vocabulary

วัด	Wâd	Monastery, Bud-
		dhist temple
โบสถ์	Bòd	temple
ทำด้วย	Tam-dûay	made of
หินอ่อน	Hǐn-àwn	marble

จาก	Jàg	from
อิตาลี	Ì-t a-li	Italy
สวย	Sǔay	beautiful
มาก	Mâg	very
จริง ๆ	Jing-jing	indeed, really
อะไร	À-rai	what
อยู่	Yù	is, are
ใน	Nai	in
นั้น	Nân	that
พระพุทธรูป	Prâ Pûd-tâ-rûb	Buddha images
น่าสนใจ	Nâ-sǒn-jai	interesting
พระสงฆ์	Prâ-sǒng	Buddhist monks
จำนวน	Jam-nuan	number
เป็นจำนวนมาก	Pen-jam-nuan Mâg	a great number of
โดยเฉพาะ	Doy-chà-pâw	especially
ระหว่าง	Râ-wàng	during
เข้าพรรษา	Kâo-pan-sǎ	the Buddhist Lent
ว่า	Wâ	say, said
หมายถึง	Mǎy-tǔeng	mean
อะไร	À-rai	what
ช่วง	Chûang	period
ประจำ	Prà-jam	permanently
อยู่ประจำ	Yù-prà-jam	stay permanently
ท่าน	Tân	he, they (to refer to monks with respect)
ค้างแรม	Káng-raem	stay overnight

ที่อื่น	Tî ùen	somewhere else, anywhere else
เดือน	Duean	month
ตั้งแต่	Tâng-tàe	since, from
ถึง	Tŭeng	to
กรกฎาคม	Gaw-râ-gà-da-kom	July
กันยายน	Gan-ya-yon	September
ทำ	Tam	do
ศึกษา	Sùeg-sǎ	study
ธรรมะ	Tam-mâ	Dhamma, Lord Buddha's Teachings
คำสั่งสอน	Kam-sàng-sǎwn	teachings
พระพุทธเจ้า	Prâ Pûd-tâ-jâo	Lord Buddha
ปฏิบัติ	Pà-tì-bàd	practice
ตาม	Tam	accordingly
นอกจากนี้	Nâwg-jàg-ní	in addition
ดูแล	Du-lae	take care
บริเวณ	Baw-rî-wen	compound
พระพุทธศาสนา	Prâ Pûd-tâ-sàd-sà-nǎ	Buddhism
รู้เรื่อง	Rú-rûeang	know about
มากกว่า	Mâg-gwà	more
เข้าไป	Kâo-pai	enter, go into
ข้างใน	Kâng-nai	inside
กรุณา	Gà-rû-na	please
บัตร	Bàd	ticket, card

ประตู	Prà-t u	door
บัตรผ่านประตู	Bàd-pàn-prà-t u	admission ticket
ผ่าน	Pàn	pass
พา...มา	Pa...Ma	take...to
ไม่เป็นไร	Mâi Pen-rai	never mind
นิดหน่อย	Nîd-nàwy	just a little
เท่านั้น	Tâo-nán	only
ก่อน	Gàwn	first
ตรงนี้	Trong-ní	right here
ถ่ายรูป	Tày-rǔb	take pictures
มุม	Mum	angle, corner
แต่งตัว	T àeng-t ua	dressed
แต่งตัวดี	T àeng-t ua Di	dressed well
รูป	Rûb	picture, photo
ออกมา	Àwg-ma	come out
น่ารัก	Nâ-râg	pretty
สำหรับ	Sǎm-ràb	for
คำชม	Kam-chom	compliments
อย่างเดียว	Yàng-diaw	only, just
พอ	Paw	enough
ก็	Gâw	just
โอ้โฮ	Ô-ho!	wow!
กลัว	Glua	afraid

3. หลักไวยากรณ์ / Làg Wai-ya-gawn / Grammar Points

1) **กรุณา** Gà-rû-na = please, a polite request. Alternate words are "Choen" and "Prod", as in the following examples:

(1) กรุณามาทางนี้

Gà-rû-na Ma Tang-nî.

Please come this way.

(2) โปรดเข้ามาข้างใน

Pròd Kâo-ma Kâng-nai.

Please come inside.

(3) เชิญเข้ามาข้างใน

Choen Kâo-ma Kâng-nai.

Please come inside.

(4) กรุณาเข้ามาข้างใน

Gà-rû-na Kâo-ma Kâng-nai.

Please come inside.

(5) เชิญมาทางนี้

Choen Ma Tang-nî.

Please come this way.

(6) โปรดมาแต่เช้า

Pròd Ma T àe-cháo.

Please come early.

2) เดือน Duean = month. The months of the year are as follows:

มกราคม	Môg-gà-ra-kom	January
กุมภาพันธ์	Gum-pa-pan	February
มีนาคม	Mi-na-kom	March
เมษายน	Me-să-yon	April
พฤษภาคม	Prûed-sà-pa-kom	May
มิถุนายน	Mî-tù-na-yon	June
กรกฎาคม	Gaw-râ-gà-da-kom	July

สิงหาคม	Sĭng-hǎ-kom	August
กันยายน	Gan-ya-yon	September
ตุลาคม	Tù-la-kom	October
พฤศจิกายน	Prûed-sà-jì-ga-yon	November
ธันวาคม	Tan-wa-kom	December

4. แบบฝึกหัด / Bàeb-fùeg-hàd / Exercises

1) Practice saying the following words:

วัด	Wâd	monastery, temple
โบสถ์	Bòd	temple
พระสงฆ์	Prâ-sŏng	Buddhist monk
พระพุทธรูป	Prâ Pûd-tâ-rûb	Buddha image
พระพุทธเจ้า	Prâ Pûd-tâ-jâo	Lord Buddha
พระพุทธศาสนา	Prâ Pûd-tâ-sàd-sà-nǎ	Buddhism
ธรรมะ	Tam-mâ	Dhamma, Lord Buddha's Teachings
คำสั่งสอน	Kam-sàng-sǎwn	teachings
เข้าพรรษา	Kâo Pan-sǎ	the Buddhist Lent

2) Practice saying the following words:

ทำด้วย	Tam-dûay	made of
หินอ่อน	Hĭn-àwn	marble
โดยเฉพาะ	Doy-chà-pâw	especially
ค้างแรม	Kâng-raem	stay overnight
ตั้งแต่	Tâng-t àe	since, from
ศึกษา	Sùeg-sǎ	study
ปฏิบัติ	Pà-tì-bàd	practice

นอกจากนี้	Nâwg-jàg-ní	in addition
ดูแล	Du-lae	take care
นิดหน่อย	Nîd-nàwy	just a little
ทางนี้	Tang-ní	this way
ถ่ายรูป	Tày-rûb	take a picture
ตรงนี้	Trong-ní	right here
ออกมา	Àwg-ma	come out
น่ารัก	Nâ-râg	pretty
คำชม	Kam-chom	compliments

3) Practice saying the following months:

กุมภาพันธ์	Gum-pa-pan	February
เมษายน	Me-să-yon	April
มิถุนายน	Mî-tù-na-yon	June
กันยายน	Gan-ya-yon	September
พฤศจิกายน	Prûed-sà-jì-ga-yon	November
มกราคม	Môg-gà-ra-kom	January
มีนาคม	Mi-na-kom	March
พฤษภาคม	Prûed-sà-pa-kom	May
กรกฎาคม	Gaw-râ-gà-da-kom	July
สิงหาคม	Sĭng-hă-kom	August
ตุลาคม	Tù-la-kom	October
ธันวาคม	Tan-wa-kom	December

4) Practice saying the following dialogue:

(1) ก: เดือนมีนาคมมีกี่วัน

Duean Mi-na-kom Mi Gì Wan?

How many days are there in March?

ข: เดือนมีนาคมมีสามสิบเอ็ดวัน

Duean Mi-na-kom Mi Săm-sìb-èd Wan.

March has 31 days.

(2) ก: เดือนเมษายนมีกี่วัน

Duean Me-să-yon Mi Gì Wan?

How many days are there in April?

ข: เดือนเมษายนมีสามสิบวัน

Duean Mè-să-yon Mi Sam-sìb Wan.

April has 30 days.

(3) ก: คุณเกิดเดือนอะไร

Kun Gòed Duean À-rai?

In which month were you born?

ข: ผมเกิดเดือนธันวาคม

Pom Gòed Duean Tan-wa-kom

I was born in December.

(4) ก: เดือนกุมภาพันธ์มีกี่วัน

Duean Gum-pa-pan Mi Gì Wan?

How many days are there in February?

ข: เดือนกุมภาพันธ์มียี่สิบแปดวันหรือยี่สิบเก้าวัน

Duean Gum-pa-pan Mi Yî-sìb-p àed Rŭe Yi-sìb-gâo Wan.

February has 28 or 29 days.

(5) ก: คุณพูดภาษาไทยได้ดีมาก

Kun Pûd Tai Dâi Di Mâg.

You can speak Thai very well.

ข: ขอบคุณสำหรับคำชม

Kàwb-kun Săm-ràb Kam-chom.

Thank you for your compliments.

5) Practice saying the following sentences:

(1) Ní Kue Wâd Ben-jà-mâ-baw-pîd.

(2) Bòd Tam-dûay Hǐn-àwn Jàg Prà-têd Ì-t a-li.

(3) Sǔay Mâg Jing-jing.

(4) A-rai Yù Nai Nán?

(5) Mi Prâ Pûd-tâ-rûb Nâ-sǒn-jai.

(6) Lâe Mi Prâ-sǒng Yù Pen-jam-nuan Mâg.

(7) Doy-chà-pâw Ra-wàng Kâo-pan-sǎ.

(8) Kun Wâ À-rai Nâ?

(9) Kâo-pan-sǎ Mǎy-tǔeng À-rai?

(10) Pen Chûang Tî Prâ-sǒng T âwng Yù Prà-jam Tî Wâd.

(11) Tân Pai Káng-raem Tî Ùen Mâi Dâi Prà-man Sǎm Duean.

(12) Tân Jà Sùeg-sǎ Tam-mâ, Lâe Pà-tì-bàd T am Kam-sàng-sǎwn.

(13) Nâwg-jàg-ní Tân Jà Chûay Du-lae Baw-rî-wen Wâd.

(14) Prâ Pûd-tâ-sàd-sà-nǎ Nâ-sǒn-jai Mâg.

(15) Pûag-rao Yàg Rú-rûeang Mâg-gwa Ní.

(16) Rao Kâo Pai Kâng-nai Bòd Dâi Mâi?

(17) Gà-rû-na Raw Prà-dǐaw.

(18) Pom Pai Súe Bàd-pàn-prà-t u Gàwn.

(19) Hai Pûag-rao Súe Dâi Mǎi?

(20) Kun Pa Pûag-rao Ma Tî-nî.

(21) Mâi Pen-rai.

(22) Nîd-nàwy Tâo-nán.

(23) Choen Ma Tang Ní.

(24) Kun Jà Tày-rûb Trong-ní Gàwn Gâw Dâi.

(25) Hâi Pǒm Tày-rûb Kun dûay.

(26) Mum Ní Sǔay Mâg Tâ Mi Kun Yù Dûay.

(27) Kun T àeng-t ua Di.

(28) Rûb Jà Àwg-ma Nâ-râg.

(29) Kàwb-kun Sǎm-ràb Kam-chom.

(30) Choen Tày-rûb Bòd Yàng-diaw Gâw Paw.

(31) Ti-ní Choen Kâo Pai Kâng-nai.

(32) Mi Prâ Pûd-tâ-rûb Mâg Jing-jing.

(33) Pǒm Glua Wâ Fim Jà Mâi Paw Tày-rûb Tî-nî.

| บทที่ 9 | Bòd Tî-gâo | The Ninth Lesson |
| นั่งตุ๊ก ๆ | Nâng Túg-túg | Ride in a Tuk-tuk |

1. บทสนทนา / Bòd Sŏn-tâ-na / Conversation

1) ก: ตุ๊ก ๆ มาแล้ว เรานั่งตุ๊ก ๆ กันดีไหม

Túg-túg Ma Láew. Rao Nâng Túg-túg Gan-di-măi?

The tuk-tuk has come. Shall we ride (in) a tuk-tuk?

ข: พวกคุณอยากจะไปไหนครับ

Pûag-kun Yàg-ja Pai Năi Krâb?

Where do you want to go, sir?

2) ก: ไม่ทราบเลย พวกเราเพิ่งมาถึงเมืองไทย

Mâi Sâb Loey. Pûag-rao Pôeng Ma-tŭeng Mueang-tai.

(We) don't know at all. We've just arrived in Thailand.

ข: ผมจะขับพาพวกคุณไปตามถนนนี้

Pŏm Jà Kàb Pa Pûag-kun Pai Tam Tà-nŏn Ní.

I will drive you along this road.

3) ก: คุณจะพาพวกเราไปถึงไหน พวกเราไม่อยากไปไกล
มากเกินไป

Kun Jà Pa Pûag-rao Pai-tŭeng Nǎi? Pûag-rao Mâi Yàg
Pai Glai Mâg.

Where will you take us to (reach)? We don't want to go
very far.

ข: งั้นไปถึงศูนย์การค้าใกล้ที่สุด ประมาณสามกิโลเมตร

Ngán Pai-tŭeng Sŭn-gan-ká Glâi Tî-sùd, Prà-man Sǎm
Gì-lo-mêd

Then (we'll go to) the nearest shopping center, about
three kilometers (from here).

4) ก: ศูนย์การค้าอะไรใกล้ที่สุด ดีเหมือนกันเราจะได้ซื้อ
ของฝาก

Sŭn-gan-ká À-rai Glâi Ti-sùd? Di Mŭean-gan Rao Jà Dâi
Súe kǎwng-fàg.

What shopping center is the nearest? (It's) good (that)
we can buy gifts.

ข: มีหลายแห่งอยู่ใกล้กัน และมีสินค้าขายมากมาย

Mi Lǎy Hàeng Yù Glâi Gan. Lâe Mi Sĭn-ká Kǎy Mâg-may.

There are many places near one another. And there are
plenty of goods for sale.

5) ก: ราคาเท่าไร รอพวกเราหนึ่งชั่วโมง และพาพวกเรากลับ
ที่เดิม

Ra-ka Tâo-rai? Raw Pûag-rao Nùeng Chûa-mong, Lâe

Pa Pûag-rao Glàb Tî Doem.

What is the price? Wait for us one hour, and take us back to the same place.

ข: แปดสิบบาทเท่านั้น แต่ผมขอโทษผมรอพวกคุณไม่ได้

P àed-sìb Bàd Tâo-nán. T àe Pǒm Kǎw-tôd Pǒm Raw Pûag-kun Mâi Dâi.

Only eighty baht. But I am sorry I can't wait for you.

6) ก: ราคาสูงไป คุณลดบ้างได้ไหม

Ra-ka Sǔng Pai. Kun Lôd Bâng Dâi Mǎi?

The price is too high. Can you lower (it) some?

ข: ไม่ได้ครับ ราคาไม่แพงเลย

Mâi Dâi Krâb. Ra-ka Mâi Paeng Loey.

No, sir. The price is not expensive at all.

7) ก: ไปเถอะ ทุกคนเชิญขึ้นนั่ง กรุณาขับช้า ๆ

Pai Tòe! Tûg Kon Choen Kûen-nâng. Gà-rû-na Kàb Chá-chá.

Let's go! Everybody please get in. Please drive slowly.

ข: ครับ ผมขับช้าเสมอ คุณนั่งสบาย ไม่ต้องห่วง

Krâb, Pǒm Kàb Chá Sà-mǒe. Kun Nâng Sà-bay. Mâi-tâwng Hùang.

Yes, I always drive slowly. You ride comfortably. Don't worry.

2. คำศัพท์ / Kam-sàb / Vocabulary

นั่ง	Nâng	ride (vehicle), sit
ตุ๊ก ๆ	Túg-túg	Thailand's popular three-wheel taxi, with noisy 'tuk-tuk' sounds

มาแล้ว	Ma-láew	have arrived
อยากจะ, อยาก	Yàg-jà, Yàg	want, would like to
ไป	Pai	go
ไหน	Năi	where
ทราบ	Sâb	know
เพิ่ง	Pôeng	just
มาถึง	Ma-tŭeng	arrive
เมืองไทย	Mueang-tai	Thailand
ขับ	Kàb	drive
ไปตาม	Pai T am	go along
ขับไปตาม	Kàb Pai Tam	drive along
ถนน	Tà-nŏn	road, street
ไปถึง	Pai-tŭeng	arrive, reach
ไปไกล	Pai Glai	go far
เกินไป	Goen-pai	too
งั้น	Ngán	then
ศูนย์การค้า	Sŭn-gan-ká	shopping center
ใกล้ที่สุด	Glâi Tî-sùd	the nearest
ดี	Di	good
เหมือนกัน	Mŭean-gan	as well
ได้	Dâi	can
ซื้อ	Súe	buy
ได้ซื้อ	Dâi Súe	can buy
ของฝาก	Kăwng-fàg	souvenir, gift
ใกล้กัน	Glâi gan	near one another
สินค้า	Sĭn-ká	goods
ขาย	Kăy	sell

มากมาย	Mâg-may	plenty
รอ	Raw	wait
พา...กลับ	Pa....Glàb	take...back
ที่เดิม	Tî Doem	the same place
แปดสิบ	P àed-sìb	eighty
บาท	Bàd	baht, Thai currency unit
ขอโทษ	Kǎw-tôd	sorry, excuse
ผมขอโทษ	Pǒm Kǎw-tôd	I'm sorry
ราคา	Ra-ka	price
สูง	Sǔng	high
ไป, เกินไป	Pai, Goen-pai	too
ลด	Lôd	discount, lower (the price)
บ้าง	Bâng	some
ไม่แพง	Mâi-paeng	inexpensive
ไปเถอะ	Pai Tòe	Let's go
ทุกคน	Tûg Kon	everybody, every person
เชิญ	Choen	please
ขึ้นนั่ง	Kûen-nâng	get in (a car, a tuk-tuk)
กรุณา	Gà-rû-na	please
ขับ	Kàb	drive
ช้า ๆ	Chá-chá	slowly
สบาย	Sà-bay	comfortable, comfortably

เสมอ	Sá-mŏe	always
ห่วง	Hùang	worry
ไม่ต้องห่วง	Mâi T âwng Hùang	don't worry

3. หลักไวยากรณ์ / Làg Wai-ya-gawn / Grammar Points

1) กันดีไหม Gan-di-mǎi = shall we, used in a suggestion; the other words used alternatively are 'Gan-mai' and 'Di-mai', as in the following examples:

(1) เรานั่งตุ๊ก ๆ กันดีไหม

Rao Nâng Túg-túg Gan-di-mǎi?

Shall we ride in a tuk-tuk?

(2) เรานั่งตุ๊ก ๆ กันไหม

Rao Nâng Túg-túg Gan-mǎi?

Shall we ride in a tuk-tuk?

(3) เรานั่งตุ๊ก ๆ ดีไหม

Rao Nâng Túg-túg Di-mǎi?

Shall we ride in a tuk-tuk?

(4) เราไปแท็กซี่กันดีไหม

Rao Pai Táeg-sî Gan-di-mǎi?

Shall we go by taxi?

(5) เราไปเดี๋ยวนี้ดีไหม

Rao Pai Dǐaw-ní Di-mǎi?

Shall we go now?

2) เถอะ Toe = Let's, used in a suggestion as well; the other word used alternatively is 'Gan-toe', as in the following examples:

(1) ไปเถอะ

Pai Tòe!   Let's go!

(2) ไปกันเถอะ

    Pai Gan-tòe!   Let us go!

(3) พวกเราไปกันเถอะ

    Pûag-rao Pai Gan-tòe!   Let us go!

(4) กินเถอะ

    Gin Tòe!

    Let's eat!

(5) กินกันเถอะ ผมหิวแล้ว

    Gin Gan-tòe! Pǒm Hǐw Láew.

    Let's eat! I'm hungry already.

(6) พวกเรากินกันเถอะ ทุกคนหิวแล้ว

    Pûag-rao Gin Gan-tòe! Tûg Kon Hǐw Láew.

    Let us eat! Everybody is hungry.

4. แบบฝึกหัด / Bàeb-fùeg-hàd / Exercises

1) Practice saying the following words:

มาแล้ว	Ma Láew	have come
ดีไหม	Di-mǎi	shall we
เพิ่งจะ	Pôeng-jà	just
เพิ่งมา	Pôeng Ma	have just come
เมืองไทย	Mueang-tai	Thailand
ไปถึง	pai-tǔeng	reach, arrive
ประมาณ	Prà-man	about, approximately
ชั่วโมง	Chûa-mong	hour
ที่เดิม	Tî-doem	the same place
แปดสิบ	P àed-sìb	eighty

เท่านั้น	Tâo-nán	only
สูงเกินไป	Sŭng Goen-pai	too high
ไม่แพงเลย	Mâi Paeng Loey	not expensive at all
ขับช้าๆ	Kàb Chá-chá	drive slowly
นั่งสบาย	Nâng Sà-bay	ride comfortably
ไม่ต้องห่วง	Mâi Tâwng Hùang	don't worry

2) Practice saying the following words:

นั่ง	Nâng	sit, ride (vehicle)
ยืน	Yuen	stand
เดิน	Doen	walk
ขับ	Kàb	drive
รอ	Raw	wait
ลด	Lôd	discount
สั้น	Sân	short
ยาว	Yaw	long
ใกล้	Glâi	near
ไกล	Glai	far
ถูก	Tùg	cheap
แพง	Paeng	expensive
ช้า	Chá	slow
เร็ว	Rew	quick, fast
หิว (ข้าว)	Hĭw (Kâw)	hungry
หิวน้ำ	Hĭw Nám	thirsty

3) Practice saying the following dialogue:

(1) ก: เราไปกันเดี๋ยวนี้ดีไหม

Rao Pai Gan Dĭaw-ní Di Măi?

Let's go now, shall we?

ข: รอเดี๋ยวให้เขามาก่อน

Raw Dĭaw. Hâi Kăo Ma Gàwn.

Wait just a minute. Let him come first.

(2) ก: เขามาแล้ว ไปกันเถอะ

Kăo Ma Láew. Pai Gan-tòe.

He has come already. Let's go!

ข: เรานั่งตุ๊ก ๆ กันดีไหม

Rao Nâng Túg-túg Gan-di-măi?

Shall we ride in a tuk-tuk?

(3) ก: เราเดินไปเถอะ

Rao Doen Pai Tòe!

Let us walk!

ข: ผมเดินไกลไม่ได้

Pŏm Doen Glai Mâi Dâi.

I can't walk far.

(4) ก: งั้นไปแท๊กซี่กันไหม

Ngán Pai Táeg-sî Gan-măi?

Shall we go by taxi then?

ข: ครับไปแท๊กซี่ดีกว่า

Krâb, Pai Táeg-sî Di-gwà.

Yes, better go by taxi.

(5) ก: แวะร้านนี้ก่อนดีไหม

Wâe Rán Ní Gàwn Di-măi?

Shall we drop in this shop first?

ข: แวะร้านนั้นเถอะ

Wâe Rán Nán Tòe.

Let's drop in that shop!

(6) ก: กลับเถอะ เราอยู่ที่นี่นานแล้ว

Glàb Tòe! Rao Yù Tî-nî Nan Láew.

Let's go back! We have been here long.

ข: นั่งอีกสักครู่ดีไหม

Nâng Ìg Sàg-krû Di-mǎi?

Shall we sit a little while more?

4) Practice saying the following sentences:

(1) Rao Nâng Túg-túg Gan-di-mǎi?

(2) Pûag-kun Yàg Pai Nǎi Krâb?

(3) Mâi Sâb Loey.

(4) Pûag-rao Pôeng Ma-tǔeng Mueang-tai.

(5) Pǒm Jà Kàb Pa Pûag-kun Pai T am Tà-nǒn Ní.

(6) Kun Jà Pa Pûag-rao Pai-tǔeng Nǎi?

(7) Pûag-rao Mâi Yàg Pai Glai Mâg.

(8) Ngán Pai-tǔeng Sǔn-gan-ká Glâi Tî-sùd, Prà-man Sǎm Gì-lo-mêd.

(9) Raw Pûag-rao Nùeng Chûa-mong.

(10) Lâe Pa Pûag-rao Glàb Tî Doem.

(11) P àed-sìb Bàd Tâo-nán.

(12) Ra-ka Sǔng Pai.

(13) Kun Lôd Bâng Dâi Mǎi?

(14) Ra-ka Mâi Paeng Loey.

(15) Pai Tòe! Tûg Kon Choen Kûen-nâng.

(16) Gà-rû-na Kàb Chá-chá.

(17) Krâb, Pǒm Kàb Chá sà-mǒe.

(18) Kun Nàng Sà-bay.

(19) Mâi-t âwng Hùang.

บทที่ 10   **Bòd Tî-sìb**   **The Tenth Lesson**
ซื้อผ้าไหมไทย   **Súe Pâ-măi Tai**   **Buying Thai Silk**

1. บทสนทนา / **Bòd Sŏn-tâ-na** / **Conversation**

1)   ก: ผมอยากซื้อผ้าไหมไทยไปฝากภรรยา   ผมควรไปซื้อที่
ไหน

Pŏm Yàg Súe Pâ-măi Tai Pai Fàg Pan-ya. Pŏm Kuan Pai
Súe Tî-năi?

I'd like to buy Thai silk for my wife. Where should I go?

ข: **แถวนี้มีหลายร้าน แต่ร้านที่ผมเคยไปซื้ออยู่ในซอย**

Tăew Ní Mi Lăy Rán. T àe Rán Tî Pŏm Koey Pai Súe Yù
Nai Sawy.

There are many shops in this neighborhood. But (the
place) where I used to go to buy (silk) is in the lane.

2) ก: ร้านชื่ออะไร อยู่ไกลไหม

Rán Chûe À-rai? Yù Glai Mǎi?

What's the name of the shop? Is it far?

ข: นี่นามบัตรชื่อร้าน อยู่ไม่ไกลจากที่นี่

Nî Nam-bàd Chûe Rán. Yù Mâi Glai Jàg Tî-nî.

Here's the shop name-card. (It's) not far from here.

3) ก: ชื่อคุ้นหูมาก คงเป็นที่รู้จักสำหรับชาวต่างประเทศและคนไทย

Chûe Kún-hǔ Mâg. Kong Pen-tî-rú-jàg Sǎm-ràb Chawt àng-prà-têd Lâe Kon Tai.

The name is very familiar. It would be well-known to foreigners and Thai people.

ข: ครับร้านมีชื่อเสียงมาก ใครๆ รู้จักดี สินค้าราคาไม่แพง และบริการดี

Krâb, Rán Mi-chûe-sǐang Mâg. Krai-krai Rú-jàg-di. Sǐn-ká Ra-ka Mâi Paeng Lâe Baw-râ-gan Di.

Yes, the shop is very famous. Anyone knows (it) well. The goods are inexpensive and service is good.

4) ก: เราน่าจะไปรถแท็กซี่ นี่แท็กซี่มีเตอร์มาแล้ว

Rao Nâ-jà Pai Rôd Táeg-sî. Nî Táeg-sî-mi-tôe Ma Láew.

We'd better go by taxi. Here comes a taxi-meter (i.e., taxi with meter).

ข: ครับเชิญขึ้นนั่งได้เลย คุณขึ้นก่อน ผมจะตามคุณ

Krâb, Choen Kûen Nâng Dâi Loey. Kûn Kuen Gawn. Pǒm Jà Tam Kun.

Yes, please just get in. You go first. I'll follow you.

5) ก: เรามาถึงร้านแล้วหรือ ให้ผมจ่ายค่าแท็กซี่นะครับ

Rao Ma-tŭeng Rán Láew Rŭe? Hâi Pŏm Jày Kâ Táeg-
sî Nâ Krâb.

Have we arrived at the shop? Let me pay for the taxi fare,

please.

ข: ไม่ต้องครับ ผมขอจ่ายค่าแท๊กซี่เอง

Mâi-tâwng Krâb. Pŏm Kăw Jày Kâ Táeg-sî Eng.

No sir, I'd like to pay for the taxi fare myself.

6) ก: ร้านใหญ่มากเหลือเกิน แผนกผ้าไหมอยู่ที่ไหน

Rán Yài Mâg Lŭea-goen. Pà-nàeg Pâ-măi Yù Tî-năi?

The shop is so large. Where's the silk department?

ข: อยู่ทางขวามือนี่ คุณบอกคนขายตรงนั้นได้เลย

Yù Tang Kwă-mue Nî. Kun Bàwg Kon-kăy Trong Nán Dâi

Loey.

(It) is here on your right. You can tell the salesgirl over

there.

7) ก: ผมต้องการซื้อผ้าไหมสีแดงหกหลาสำหรับภรรยา
และเสื้อเชิร์ตสีเทา สองตัวสำหรับผมเอง

Pŏm Tâwng-gan Súe Pâ-măi Sĭ-daeng Hòg Lă Săm-ràb

Pan-ya. Lâe Sûea Chóed Sĭ-tao Săwng T ua Săm-ràb

Pŏm Eng.

I'd like to buy six yards of red silk cloth for my wife. And

two gray shirts for myself.

ข: ทำไมคุณไม่ซื้อเสื้อเชิร์ตสีเทาและสีฟ้าอย่างละตัว ทั้ง
สองสีเหมาะสำหรับคุณใส่ไปทำงาน

Tam-mai Kun Mâi Súe Sûea Chóed Sĭ-tao Lâe Sĭ-fá

Yàng-lâ T ua? Táng Săwng Sĭ Màw Săm-ràb Kun Sài

Pai Tam-ngan.

Why don't you buy (one) gray and (one) light blue shirt
each? Both colors are fit for you to wear to work.

2. คำศัพท์ / Kam-sàb / Vocabulary

ผ้าไหม	Pâ-mai	silk, silk cloth
ผ้าไหมไทย	Pâ-mǎi Tai	Thai silk
อยากซื้อ	Yàg Súe	would like to buy
ไปฝาก	Pai Fàg	for a gift
แถวนี้	Tǎew Ní	this neighborhood
เคยไปซื้อ	Koey Pai Súe	used to go to buy
ซอย	Sawy	lane, alley
ชื่อ	Chûe	name
นามบัตร	Nam-bàd	name card
ชื่อร้าน	Chûe Rán	shop name
คุ้นหู	Kún-hǔ	familiar
คง	Kong	might
เป็นที่รู้จัก	Pen-tî-rú-jàg	well-known
สำหรับ	Sǎm-ràb	for
ชาวต่างประเทศ	Chaw-t àng-prà-têd	foreigner
คนไทย	Kon Tai	Thai people
มีชื่อเสียง	Mi-chûe-sǐang	famous
ใคร ๆ	Krai-krai	anyone, someone
รู้จักดี	Rú-jàg-di	well-known, know well
สินค้า	Sǐn-ká	goods
ราคา	Ra-ka	price
ไม่แพง	Mâi Paeng	not expensive

บริการ	Baw-rî-gan	service
บริการดี	Baw-rî-gan Di	good service
น่าจะ	Nâ-jà	had better
แท๊กซี่มีเตอร์	Táeg-sî-mi-tôe	taxi-meter
ขึ้น ขึ้นนั่ง	Kûen, Kûen-nâng	just get in, get in
ก่อน	Gàwn	first
ตาม	Tam	follow
ค่าแท๊กซี่	Kâ Táeg-sî	taxi fare
ไม่ต้อง	Mâi-tâwng	don't, no
ใหญ่มาก	Yài Mâg	very large
เหลือเกิน	Lŭea-goen	so
ใหญ่มากเหลือเกิน	Yài Mâg Lŭea-goen	so large
แผนก	Pà-nàeg	department
แผนกผ้าไหม	Pà-nàeg Pî-măi	silk department
ขวามือ	Kwă-mue	right hand
ซ้ายมือ	Sáy-mue	left hand
ทางขวามือ	Tang Kwă-mue	on the right hand
บอก	Bàwg	tell
คนขาย	Kon Kăy	salesgirl
ตรงนั้น	Trong Nán	over there
หกหลา	Hòg Lă	six yards
สีแดง	Sĭ-daeng	red
สีเทา	Sĭ-tao	gray
สีฟ้า	Sĭ-fá	light blue
สี	Sĭ	color
ทั้งสองสี	Táng Săwng Sĭ	both colors

เหมาะสำหรับ	Màw Sǎm-ràb	fit for
ใส่	Sài	wear, put on
ทำงาน	Tam-ngan	work
ใส่ไปทำงาน	Sài Pai Tam-ngan	wear to work

3. หลักไวยากรณ์ / Làg Wai-ya-gawn / Grammar Points

1) เคย... Koey = used to ..., and ever, "Mâi Koey" = never, as the following examples:

(1) ผมเคยไปที่ร้านอยู่ในซอย

Pǒm Koey Pai Tî Rán Yù Nai Sawy.

I used to go to the shop in the alley.

(2) พวกเราเคยมาเมืองไทยแล้วสองครั้ง

Pûag-rao Koey Ma Mueang-tai Láew Sǎwng Kráng.

We have been to Thailand twice.

(3) คุณเคยพบเขาไหม

Kun Koey Pôb Kǎo Mǎi?

Have you ever met him?

(4) เขาเคยมาเยี่ยมพวกเรา

Kǎo Koey Ma Yîam Pûag-rao.

They used to visit us.

(5) ผมไม่เคยไปเชียงใหม่

Pǒm Mâi Koey Pai Chiang-mài

I've never been to Chiang Mai.

(6) ดิฉันไม่เคยรู้จักคุณ

Dì-chân Mâi Koey Rú-jàg Kun.

I've never known you.

2) **น่าจะ** Nâ-jà = had better, but sometimes "Nâ-jà... Di-gwà" is also used alternatively. For example:

    (1) **เราน่าจะไปแท๊กซี่**

        Rao Nâ-jà Pai Táeg-sî.

        We'd better go by taxi.

    (2) **คุณน่าจะซื้อเสื้อสีฟ้า**

        Kun Nâ-jà Súe Sûea Sĭ-fá.

        You'd better buy a light blue shirt.

    (3) **พวกเราน่าจะไปพรุ่งนี้ดีกว่า**

        Pûag-rao Nâ-jà Pai Prûng-ní Di-gwà.

        We'd better go tomorrow.

    (4) **เขาน่าจะมาถึงแต่เช้า**

        Kăo Nâ-jà Ma T àe-cháo.

        He'd better come early.

    (5) **คุณน่าจะโทรมาบอกผมก่อน**

        Kun Nâ-jà To Ma Bàwg Pŏm Gàwn.

        You'd better phone to tell me first.

    (6) **พวกเขาน่าจะพักที่นี่ดีกว่า**

        Pûag-kăo Nâ-jà Pâg Tî-nî Di-gwà.

        They'd better stay here.

3) **คง..คงจะ** Kong, Kong-jà.... = would, could, etc, used in conditional sentences, as in the following examples:

    (1) **คงเป็นที่รู้จัก**

        Kong Pen-tî-rú-jàg.

        (It) would be well-known.

    (2) **เขาคงมาถึงพรุ่งนี้เช้า**

        Kao Kong Ma-tŭeng Prûng-ní Cháo.

He might arrive tomorrow morning.

(3) **พวกเราคงจะพักที่นี่อีกสองสามวัน**

Pûag-rao Kong-jà Pâg Tî-nî Ìg Săwng-săm Wan.

We would stay here a few days more.

(4) **อากาศคงจะหนาวมากกว่านี้**

A-gàd Kong-jà Năw Mâg-gwà Ní.

The weather would be much colder than this.

(5) **สินค้าที่นั่นคงจะแพงมาก**

Sĭn-ká Tî-nân Kong-jà Paeng Mâg.

The goods there would be very expensive.

(6) **พวกเราคงได้พบกันอีก**

Pûag-rao Kong Dâi Pôb Gan Ìg.

We could meet again.

(7) **คุณคงพูดภาษาไทยได้เก่งแล้ว**

Kun Kong Pûd Pa-să Tai Dâi Gèng Láew.

You could have spoken Thai well.

4) สี Sĭ = color. Some words for colors are as follows:

แดง	Daeng	red
ขาว	Kăo	white
น้ำเงิน	Nám-ngoen	blue
ฟ้า	Fá	light blue
เทา	Tao	gray
เขียว	Kĭaw	green
เหลือง	Lŭeang	yellow
น้ำตาล	Nám-tan	brown
ดำ	Dam	black
ม่วง	Mûang	purple

ชมพู	Chom-pu̲	pink
สีอ่อน	Sĭ A̲wn	light color
สีเข้ม	Sĭ Kê̲m	dark color
สีสด	Sî Sò̲d	bright color

4. แบบฝึกหัด / Bàeb-fùeg-hàd / Exercises

1) Practice saying the following words:

ซื้อ	Sú̲e	buy
ขาย	Kă̲y	sell
เคย	Ko̲ey	used to, ever
อยาก	Yà̲g	would like to, want
จ่าย	Jà̲y	pay
บอก	Bà̲wg	tell
หลา	Lă̲	yard
คง	Kong	would
แดง	Da̲eng	red
ขาว	Kă̲w	white
เทา	Tao	gray
เขียว	Kĭa̲w	green
เหลือง	Lŭe̲ang	yellow
ฟ้า	Fá̲	light blue
ขึ้น	Kûen	get in, ride, up
ลง	Long	come down, down

2) Practice saying the following words and phrases:

ผ้าไหม	Pâ̲-măi	silk, silk cloth
อยากซื้อ	Yà̲g Sú̲e	would like to buy
อยากไป	Yà̲g Pa̲i	would like to go

ควรไป	Kuan Pai	should go
แถวนี้	Tǎew Ní	this neighborhood
นามบัตร	Nam-bàd	name-card
คุ้นหู	Kún-hǔ	familiar
มีชื่อเสียง	Mi-chûe-sǐang	famous
เป็นที่รู้จัก	Pen-tî-rú-jàg	well-known
ชาวต่างประ	Chaw-tàng-prà-têd	foreigner
เทศ		
น่าจะ	Nâ-jà	had better
ใหญ่มาก	Yài Mâg	very large
คนขาย	Kon Kǎy	salesgirl
เสื้อเชิร์ต	Sûea Chóed	shirt
สีเทา	Sǐ-tao	gray
สีน้ำเงิน	Sǐ-nám-ngoen	dark blue
ทั้งสองสี	Táng Sǎwng Sǐ	both colors

3) Practice saying the following dialogue:

(1) ก: คุณอยากจะไปไหน

Kun Yàg-jà Pai Nǎi?

Where would you like to go?

ข: ผมอยากไปซื้อผ้าไหม

Pǒm Yàg Pai Súe Pâ-mǎi.

I'd like to go to buy silk cloth.

(2) ก: คุณเคยไปที่ไหนมาแล้ว

Kun Koey Pai Tî-nǎi Ma Láew?

Where have you ever been?

ข: ผมยังไม่เคยไปที่ไหนเลย

Pǒm Yang Mâi Koey Pai Tî-nǎi Loey.

I've never been anywhere yet.

(3) ก: พวกเราน่าจะไปที่ร้านนี้

Pûag-rao Nâ-jà Pai Tî Rán Ní.

We'd better go to this shop.

ข: เราคงไปไม่ได้ เพราะมันอยู่ไกลมาก

Rao Kong Pai Mâi Dâi, Prâw Man Yù Glai Mâg.

We could not (possibly) go, because it is very far.

(4) ก: พวกเราน่าจะไปแท๊กซี่

Pûag-rao Nâ-jà Pai Táeg-sî.

We'd better go by taxi.

ข: รถคงติดมากวันนี้

Rôd Kong Tìd Mâg Wan-ní.

The traffic might be very heavy today.

(5) ก: เราควรซื้อที่ร้านใกล้ที่นี่

Rao Kuan Súe Tî Rán Glâi Tî-nî.

We should buy at the shop near here.

ข: ของแถวนี้คงจะแพง

Kǎwng Tǎew-ní Kong Jà Paeng.

Things in this neighborhood might be expensive.

(6) ก: คุณน่าจะกลับพรุ่งนี้

Kun Nâ-Jà Glab Prûng-ní.

You'd better go back tomorrow.

ข: ผมควรไปตั้งแต่เมื่อวานนี้แล้ว

Pǒm Kuan Pai Tâng-t àe Mûea-wan-ní.

I should have gone since yesterday.

4) Practice saying the following sentences:

(1) Pǒm Yàg Súe Pâ-mǎi Tai Pai Fàg Pan-ya.

(2) Pŏm Kuan Pai Súe Tî-năi?

(3) Tăew Ní Mi Lăy Rán.

(4) T àe Rân Tî Pŏm Koey Pai Súe Yù Nai Sawy.

(5) Rán Chûe À-rai?

(6) Rán Yù Glai Măi?

(7) Yù Mâi Glai Jàg Tî-nî.

(8) Chûe Kún-hŭ Mâg.

(9) Kong Pen-tî-rú-jàg Săm-ràb Chaw-t àng-prà-têd Lâe Kon Tai.

(10) Rán Mi-chûe-sĭang Mâg.

(11) Krai-krai Rú-jàg Di.

(12) Sĭn-ká Ra-ka Mâi Paeng Lâe Baw-rî-gan Di.

(13) Rao Nâ-jà Pai Rôd Táeg-sî.

(14) Rao Ma-tŭeng Rán Láew Rŭe?

(15) Hâi Pŏm Jày Kâ Táeg-sî Nâ Krâb.

(16) Mâi-t âwng, Pŏm Kăw Jày Kâ Táeg-sî Eng.

(17) Rán Yài Mâg Lŭea-goen.

(18) Pà-nàeg Pâ-măi Yù Tî-năi:

(19) Yù Tang Kwă-mue Nî.

(20) Kun Bàwg Kon-kăy Trong Nán Dâi Loey.

(21) Pŏm T âwng-gan Súe Pâ-măi Hòg Lă Săm-ràb Pan-ya.

(22) Pŏm T âwng-gan Sûea Chóed Sĭ-tao Săwng T ua Săm-ràb Pŏm Eng.

(23) Pâ-măi Sĭ-daeng T àe Sûea Sĭ-tao.

(24) Tam-mai Kun Mâi Súe Sĭ-tao Lâe Sĭ-fá Yàng-lâ T ua:

(25) Táng Săwng Sĭ Màw Săm-ràb Kun Sài Pai Tam-ngan.

(26) Pŏm Châwb Táng Săwng Sĭ.

ดัชนีหลักไวยากรณ์
Dàd-châ-ni Làg Wai-ya-gawn
Grammar Points Index

คำศัพท์ไทย-อังกฤษ
Kam-sàb Tai-Ang-grìd
Thai - English Vocabulary

A-gàd weather
A-hǎn food
A-hǎn Jin Chinese food
A-hǎn Fà-ràng European food
A-hǎn Tai Thai food
A-hǎn Yî-pùn Japanese food
À-rai what
À-ràwy delicious
À-ràwy Tî-sùd most delicious
Àd, Àd-jà may
Ang-grid English
Ǎw I see, exclamation for understanding
Àwg-ma come out
Bàd card, ticket
Bàd-pàn-prà-tu admission ticket
Bàd baht, Thai currency unit
Bàeb-fùeg-hàd exercises
Bang some
Bang Wan some days
Bâng any, some

Baw-rî-gan service
Baw-rî-gan Di good service
Baw-rî-wen compound, enclosure
Bàwg tell
Bày afternoon, in the afternoon
Ben-jà-mâ-baw-pîd the Marble Temple
Bòd lesson, lessons
Bòd Sǒn-tâ-na conversation
Bòd temple
Chá slow, slowly
Chá-chá slowly
Châ-nîd kind
Châ-nîd Nǎi what kind
Châwb like
Châi yes
Châi Laew that's right
Chái use
Cháo morning
Tàe-cháo early in the morning
Chaw-tàng-prà-têd foreigner

Choen please

Choen Pai please go

Choen Kâo-ma please come in

Chim taste

Chôk-di good luck, lucky

Chom admire

Chom sà-tǎn-tî-sam-kan go sight-seeing

Chom-pu, Sǐ-chom-pu pink

Chûa-mong hour

Sǎwng Chûa-mong two hours

Chûang period

Chûay help

Chûe name

Chûe Rán shop name

Dâi can

Mâi Dâi cannot

Dam, Sǐ-dam black

Dàn Trùad-kon-kâo-mueang immigration

Dân-lǎng behind

Dang-nán...Jueng That's why, therefore

Di good

Di-gwà better

Di Láew good enough

Di-mǎi shall we

Di Ti-diaw quite good

Diaw-gan the same

Doen walk

Doen-tang travel,make a trip

Doen-tang Tàw continue traveling

Doy-chà-pâw especially

Du look, have a look

Du Sî Please look!

Du Sî Nân have a look at that

Du-lae take care

Dûay as well, also, too

Duean month

Dùeg late at night

Eng self

Fà-ràng European

Fá, Sǐ-fá light blue

Fàg give

Kǎwng-fàg gift, souvenir

Sue Fàg buy for (someone)

Fim film

Fim Lǎy Múan many rolls of film

Gà-rû-na please

Gàb with

Pai Gàb go with

Gài hen, chicken

Gan-ya-yon September

Gaw-râ-gà-da-kom July

Gâo nine

   Tî-gâo ninth

Gàwn first

   Pai Gàwn go first

Gèng good at, well

   Pûd Gèng speak well

Gì-lo-mêd kilometer

Gin eat

Glàb go back, return, leave

Glâi near, almost

Glâi-glâi near

Glâi Gan near one another

Glâi Tî-sùd nearest

Glai far

Glang-kuen night-time, at night

Glang-wan daytime

Glâwng-tày-rûb camera

Glìn smell

Glua afraid

Goen-pai, Pai too

   Paeng Pai too expensive

Mâg Pai, Mâg Goen Pai too

   much, too many

Grà-pǎo bag, luggage

Grà-pǎo Doeng-tang traveling

bag, travel luggage

Grung-têb Bangkok

Gum-pa-pan February

Hâ five

Hâ-sìb fifty

   Tî-hâ fifth

Hâwng room

Hěn see

Hì-mâ snow

   Hì-mâ Tòg it snows.

Hǐn-àwn marble

Hǐw, Hǐw Kâw hungry

Hǐw Nám thirsty

Hòg six

Hòg-sìb sixty

   Tî-hòg sixth

Hùang worry

Ì-ta-li Italy

Ìg again, else

Ìg-kráng once again

Jà will

Jà Pai will go

Jà Yù will stay

Jàg from

Jàwd park (a car)

   Lan Jàwd Rôd parking lot

   Tî Jàwd Rôd parking place

Jam-nuan number

Jam-nuan Mâg a great number

Jèd seven

  Tî-jèd seventh

  Jèd-sìb seventy

Jing-jing indeed, really

Jin Chinese

Kâ yes, sir, madam; please (used by females)

Kâ Tâeg-sî taxi fare

Kà-nǔn jackfruit

Kàb drive (a car)

Kàb Pai T am drive along

Kàeg guest

Kài eggs

Kam dark

Kam-sàb vocabulary

Kam-chom compliments

Kam-sàng-sǎwn teachings

Kâng beside

Kâng-nai inside

Káng-raem stay overnight

Kâo towards, enter

Kâo-chom visit

Kâo-pai go into, enter

Kâo-pan-sǎ Buddhist Lent

Kǎw, Sǐ-Kâw white

Kâo rice

Kǎw let, May I

Kǎw T âwn-râb welcome to

Kǎw-tôd sorry, excuse

  Pǒm Kǎw-tôd I'm sorry

Kàwb-kun thank you, thanks

Kǎwng of

Kǎwng-dì-chǎn my (used by females)

Kǎwng-fàg souvenir, gift

Kǎwng-kǎo his, her

Kǎwng-pûag-kǎo their

Kǎwng-kun your

Kǎwng-man its

Kǎwng-pǒm my

Kǎwng-rao our

Kǎy sell

Kǐaw, Sǐ-kǐaw green

Kid charge (money)

Koey used to, ever

  Mâi Koey never

Koey Pai used to go

Kǒn carry

Kon person, people

Kon-kǎy salesgirl

Kon Tai Thai, Thai people

Kong, Kong-jà might, would,

could

Krâb yes, sir, madam; please (used by males)

Krai who

Krai-krai anyone, someone

Krûeng half

  Krûeng Chûa-mong half an hour

Kuan should

Kue is

Kûen get on (a bus), get in (a car)

Kûen-nâng get on for a ride

Kuen night

Kun you

Kún-hǔ familiar

Kwǎ-mue right hand

  Sáy-mue left hand

Lǎ yard

Láew already, then

Làg Wai-ya-gawn grammar points

Lan open space

  Lan-jàwd-rôd parking lot, parking space

Lán million

  Hâ-lán five million

Lǎng, Lǎng-jàg after

Lawng try

Lǎy many

Loey ahead

  Mâi... Loey not at all

  Mâi Châwb Loey don't like it at all

Lôd discount, lower the price

Long-ma come down

Long-ma Láew has come down

Lǔea-goen so

  Mag Lǔea-goen so many

Luem forget

Luem...Wái leave, left

Lǔeang, Sǐ-lǔeang yellow

Nâ next

  Sàb-da Nâ next week

  Wan-jan Nâ next Monday

Nâ-jà had better

Nà-sǒn-jai interesting

Nâ-râg pretty

Na-ti minute

Nâe-nam recommend, suggest

Nai in

Nǎi where, anywhere

Na-lî-ga watch, o'clock, hour

Nám water

Năm spine, thorn

  Mi-năm spiny

Nam-bàd name card

Nám-ng<u>oen</u>, Sĭ-nám-ng<u>oen</u>, blue

Nám-t<u>an</u>, Sĭ-nám-t<u>an</u> brown

Nán that

N<u>an</u> long (time)

Nan-n<u>an</u> for a long time

Năng-s<u>ŭe</u>-d<u>oen</u>-tang passport

Nâng sit, ride (a vehicle)

Náwy little

Năw cold

Năw-gwà colder

Nâw<u>g</u>-jàg-nî in addition

Nàwy-nâ please

Ngan then

Nî, Tî-nî here, this place

Nî this

Nîd-nàwy just a little

Nùeng one

  Tî-nùeng first

Nùeng Tûm seven o'clock in the evening, 7 PM

Ma come

Ma Láew have come

Ma-tŭeng reach, arrive (towards the speaker)

Má horse

Mă dog

Mâ-r<u>uen</u>-nî the day after tomorrow

Ma-yîam visit

Mâg many, much, very

Mâg-may plenty

Mâg Tâo-rai how much

Mâg-mâg very much

Mâg Tî-sud most

Mâg-gwà more

Mă i question word, yes/no answers

Mă i silk

Mài again, new

Mâi not, no

Mâi Châwb do not know

Mâi Châwb Loey don't like at all

Mâi Dâi cannot

Mâi Glai not far

Mâi Koey never

Mâi Mòd not all

Mâi Paeng not expensive

Mâi-Paeng inexpensive

Mâi Pen-rai never mind, that's O.K.

Mâi-t âwng don't, no, no need to

Mâi-t âwng Huang Don't worry

Mái wood

Mâi burn, burnt

Man it

Mang-kûd mangosteen

Màw fit, suitable

Màw Sǎm-ràb fit for

Mǎy-tǔeng mean

Měn bad (smell), smelly

Měn Tî-sùd (smell) the worst

Me-sǎ-yon April

Mî-tù-na-yon June

Mi there is/there are

Mi-chûe, Mi-chûe-sǐang famous

Mi-gǐn smell

Mi-na-kom March

Mi-nǎm spiny

Môg-gà-ra-kom January

Múan roll

Mûang, Sǐ-mûang purple

Mûea, Mûea-rai when

Mǔean-gan also, as well, too

Mueang city

Mueang-tai Thailand

Mûed dark

Mùen ten thousand

Mum angle, corner

Ô-ho Wow

Pa take

Pa...Glàb take...back

Pa...Ma take...to (this place)

Pa...Pai take...to (that place)

Pâ-mǎi silk cloth, silk

Pà-nàeg department

Pà-nàeg Pâ-mǎi silk department

Pǎen-tî map

Pâg, Pâg-yu stay

Pan thousand

Pan-ya wife

Pàn pass

Paw enough

Paw Láew just enough, enough already

Pôb meet, see

Pôb-gan meet each other, see each other

Pôb-gan Ìg see you again

Pôb-gan Mài see you again

Pôeng, Pôeng-ja just

Pôeng-jà Ma-tǔeng have just arrived

Pǒm I, me (used by males)

Pon-lâ-mái fruit

Prâ Baw-rom-mâ-hǎ Râd-châ-wang the Grand Palace

Prâ Pûd-tâ-jâo Lord Buddha

Prâ Pûd-tâ-rûb Buddha images

Prâ Pûd-tâ-sàd-sà-nǎ Buddhism

Prâ-sǒng Buddhist monks

Prâw because

Práwm ready

Práwm Jà Pai ready to go

Prûed-sà-jì-ga-yon November

Prûed-sà-pa-kom May

Prûng-ní tomorrow

Pu-gèd Phuket

Pûag-rao we, us

Pûd speak

Pûd Ang-grìd speak English, speaking English

Pûd Dâi can speak

Pûd Fà-ràng-sèd speak French, speaking French

Pûd Tai speak Thai, speaking Thai

Pûd Yî-pùn speak Japanese, speaking Japanese

Pûd Yoe-râ-man speak German, speaking German

Pà-tì-bàd practice

P àed eight

Tî-p àed eighth

P àed-sìb eighty

Pai go

Pai Di Mǎi shall we go

Pai Fàg (buy) for a gift

Pai Glai go far

Pai T am go along

Pai T àw go after (this)

Pai Tòe let's go

Pai-tùeng reach, arrive (away from the speaker)

Pen am (is, are)

Pen-jam-nuan Mag a great number of

Pen-tî-nî-yom popular

Pen-tî-rú-jàg well-known

Plàeg strange

Plàeg Di quite strange

P òed open

Prà-dǐaw a minute, just a minute

Prà-jam permanently

Prà-man about, approximate, approximately

Prà-têd country

Prà-têd Tai Thailand

Prà-t u door, gate

   Bàd-pàn-prà-t u admission ticket

Ra-ka price, fare

Râb-prà-tan have (eat)

Râb-rawng entertain, welcome

Ram dancing

Rán shop, store

Rán-a-hǎn food shop, restaurant

Rán-tày-rûb photo shop

Rao, Pûag-rao we, us

Raw wait

Ráwn hot

Ráwy hundred

   Sǎwng-ráwy two hundred

   Tî-ráwy hundredth

Rîb-ráwn hurry

Rôem start, begin

Rôd-tìd heavy traffic, traffic jam

Rôd-tìd Mâg very heavy traffic

Rong-raem hotel

Rú-jàg know

Rú-jàg-di well-known, know well

Rú-rûeang know about

Rûb picture, photo

Rûb-tày picture, photograph, photo

Rûe-du season

Rûe-du Nǎw winter, cold season

Rûe-du Ráwn summer, hot season

Rûe-du Fǒn rainy season

Rǔe question word, for yes/no answers

Sà-bay comfortable, comfortably

Sà-daeng show, showing

Sà-mǒe always

Sà-tǎn-tî place

Sà-wàd-di hello, good morning, etc.

Sà-wàng bright, daylight

Sàb-da week

Sâb know

Sǎen hundred thousand

Sái wear, put on

Sái Pai Tam-ngan wear to work

Sǎm-kan important

Sǎm-ràb for

Sǎm three

Tî-sǎm third

Sǎm-sìb thirty

Tî-sǎm-sìb thirtieth

Sàm-pan three thousand

Sân short

Sǎwng two

Tî-sǎwng second

Sǎwng-ráwy two hundred

Sǎwng-sǎm few

Sǎwng Tûm eight o'clock in the evening, 8 PM

Sǎwng Mong Cháo eight o'clock in the morning, 8 AM

Sawy lane, alley

Sǎy late in the morning, behind schedule

Sáy-mue left hand

Sìb ten

Tî-sìb tenth

Sìb-èd eleven

Tî-sìb-èd eleventh

Sìb-sǎm thirteen

Sîd-nî Sydney

Sǐn-ká goods

Sî of course; please, an ending particle for a request or command

Sǐ color

Sǐ Àwn light color

Sǐ-daeng red

Sǐ-fá light blue, sky color

Sǐ Kêm dark color

Sǐ Sòd bright color

Sǐ-tao gray

Sǐng-hǎ-kom August

Sǒn-jai interested

Sù to, towards

Sǔay beautiful

Súe buy

Súe-kǎwng shopping

Sǔn-gan-ká shopping center

Sùeg-sǎ study

Sǔng high

Sǔng Goen-pai too high

Tà-nǒn road, street

Táeg-sî taxi

Táeg-sî-mi-tôe taxi-meter

Tǎew-nî this neighborhood

Tai Thai

Tam do

Tam-dûay made of

Tam-mâ Lord Buddha's Teachings, Dhamma

Tam-ngan work

Tan-ti right away, immediately

Tan-wa-kom December

Tân he, they (to refer to monks with respect)

Táng all

Táng-mòd all, all of them

Táng-mòd Ní all of these

Táng-nán all

Táng Săwng Sĭ both colors

Táng Wan all day

Táng Wan Táng Kuen both day and night

Tang Kwă-mue on the right hand

Tao, Sĭ-tao gray

Tâo-nán only, just

Tâo-rai how much

Tày-rûb take pictures

Tî at, place

 Sà-tăn-tî place

Tî Doem the same place

Tî-năi, Năi where

Tî-nî here, this place

Tî-nán, Tî-nán that place, there

Tî-nùeng first

Tî-sùd the most

Tî Uèn somewhere else, any-

where else

Tîang, Tîang-wan noon, mid-day

Tîang-kuen midnight

Tîaw-chom tour, visit

To, To-râ-sàb phone, tel-ephone

Ton bear

Ton Mâi Dâi cannot bear

Tûg Kon every person, every-one

Tŭg cheap

Tŭrian durian, a spiny fruit with yellow meat

Tŭeng to, reach, arrive

Tŭeng Láew have arrived

T àe but

T àe-cháo early in the morning

T àe-lâ each

T àe-lâ Hàeng each place

T àeng-t ua dressed

T àeng-t ua Di dressed well

T am accordingly, follow

 Pà-tì-bàd Tam practice ac-cordingly

Tâng-t àe since, from

T âwng-gan want, would like

T âwn-ráb welcome

Tòg fall

  Hì-mâ Tòg it snows.

Tòg-long all right, O.K.

Trong-ní right here

Trong-nán over there

Tù-la-kom October

T ǔa ticket

T ǔa-krûeang-bin plane ticket

Túg-túg tuk-tuk, Thailand's popular three-wheel taxi with noisy 'tuk-tuk' sounds

Wâ say, that

  Kǎo Pûd Wâ he says that

  Kun Wâ À-rai? what did you say?

Wâd monastery, Buddhist temple

Wâd Po the Reclining Buddha Temple, Wat Pho

Wâd Prâ Gâew the Emerald Buddha Temple, Wat Phra Kaeo

Wâe drop in, stop for a short while

Wan day

  Wan-a-tîd Sunday

Wan-jan Monday

Wan-ang-kan Tuesday

Wan-pûd Wednesday

Wan-pâ-rûe-hâd-baw-di Thursday

Wan-sùg Friday

Wan-sǎo Saturday

Wan-châd national day

Wan-gòed birthday

Wan Nâ next day

Wan-kâo-pan-sǎ Buddhist Lent Day

Wan-ní today

Wan-ní yesterday

Wan Prâ Buddhist Holy Day

Wan-raeng-ngan Labor Day

Way Em Si E YMCA

We-la time

We-la Gin eating time

We-la Nawn sleeping time

We-la Tam-ngan working time

Wî-na-ti second

Win-soe Windsor

Yàg, Yàg-jà would like to

Yàg Súe would like to buy

Yài big, large

Yài Mâg very large

Yài Mâg Lŭea-goen so large

Yài Tî-sùd biggest

Yang still, yet

Yàng-diaw, just, only, one thing

Yaw long

Yî-pùn Japanese

 A-hăn Yî-pùn Japanese food

 Kon Yî-pùn Japanese people

 Pa-sa Yî-pùn Japanese language

 Pra-têd Yî-pùn Japan

Yî-sìb twenty

 Tî-yî-sìb twentieth

Yî-sìb-èd twenty-one

 Tî-yî-sìb-èd twenty-first

Yî-sìb-hâ twenty-five

 Tî-yî-sìb-hâ twenty-fifth

Yôg-wén except

Yù is (am, are), stay, live

Yù Prà-jam stay permanently

Yuen stand